# Succ
# a Head of Year

## JON TAIT

**BLOOMSBURY EDUCATION**

LONDON   OXFORD   NEW YORK   NEW DELHI   SYDNEY

BLOOMSBURY EDUCATION
Bloomsbury Publishing Plc
50 Bedford Square, London, WC1B 3DP, UK

BLOOMSBURY, BLOOMSBURY EDUCATION and the Diana logo are
trademarks of Bloomsbury Publishing Plc

First published in Great Britain 2020

ISBN: PB: 978-1-4729-6337-6; ePDF: 978-1-4729-6338-3;
ePub: 978-1-4729-6339-0

2 4 6 8 10 9 7 5 3

Typeset by Newgen KnowledgeWorks Pvt. Ltd., Chennai, India
Printed and bound in the UK by CPI Group (UK) Ltd., Croydon, CR0 4YY

MIX
Paper from
responsible sources
FSC® C013604

To find out more about our authors and books visit www.bloomsbury.com
and sign up for our newsletters

# Contents

# Acknowledgements

Back in 2003, midway through my second year in teaching, I was called to Cath Sewell's office. Cath was Assistant Headteacher at Woodham Community Technology College (now Woodham Academy) and a great mentor. I remember Cath asking me if I'd seen the internal advert for the assistant head of year job that had just been put up in the staffroom and if I had thought about it. I hadn't. In fact, I had never had any desires to do anything other than come into teaching to teach PE. I vividly remember my polite but frank response: 'Why would I want to pick up everyone else's crap all day long?' But that's just what I ended up doing for the next 16 years of my teaching career – first as that assistant head of year, then on to head of year, followed by assistant headteacher overseeing all the pastoral elements of the school, before moving on to deputy headteacher. That day changed the course of my career, gave me the opportunity to grow and learn in ways I never thought I could, and turbo-boosted my path to senior leadership. I'll always be grateful to Cath for seeing something in me that I had never seen in myself.

During my career I have been lucky enough to work with some amazing pastoral staff, from heads of year to non-teaching support staff. The commitment, energy and passion that these people have for guiding young people towards a better future is truly remarkable. I've learnt and developed my craft via 'on-the-job training' from these incredible professionals throughout my career. Whether it was how to handle a tricky parent in reception, or how to make that tough phone call that nobody wants to make, there have always been fantastic pastoral role models to look up to and learn from. Through the laughs, jokes, tears and challenging situations, we've always stuck together.

I would also like to say a huge thank you to each and every one of the 14 middle and senior leaders who answered the call on social media to contribute to this book. The professional perspectives at the end of each chapter give an authentic view from the front line, providing advice and guidance on how to put the theory into practice. Big thanks to Anna Wass, Ryan Oates, Chris Farman, Steve Hoey, Tom Smith, Joey Kock, Joe Varey, Mike O'Brien, Adele Mulligan, Jamie Wordsworth, Mark Allen, Vikki Fawcett, Jane Darbyshire and Lynette Harte. I hugely appreciate the work you all put into your respective chapter contributions, giving a great insight into the real job.

Thanks also need to go to the whole team at Bloomsbury Education for giving me the opportunity to have my writing published and supporting me through book number three. This is definitely something I never even dreamed of, or would have even thought possible as a C-grade English student at GCSE. It makes me proud to know that my writing can help teachers and leaders all over the world and that I'm able to make a difference far more widely than the four walls of my own school.

Finally, to my amazing wife Tracy and our two beautiful children Robbie and Isabelle. Writing can be a long and lonely process, shutting yourself away on weekends or evenings so you can focus your thoughts solely on your work. Without their complete support and understanding at home, none of the three books that I have written would ever have made it to print. Tracy has supported not only my writing but my career aspirations as well. Her commitment to our children has sometimes meant putting her own career aspirations in education on hold in order to support mine, whilst putting the needs of our family first. For this, the children and I will be eternally grateful.

# Introduction

This book has been written for current and aspiring heads of year, together with anyone looking to move into a pastoral middle leadership role at school. It has been written from my own personal experience of working my way through the pastoral leadership system, starting out as an assistant head of year and moving up to head of year through to senior leadership roles as an assistant headteacher and then deputy headteacher responsible for pastoral care. I've tried to piece together all the knowledge and experience that I have developed over the past 16 years in pastoral care and put it into a guidebook that you can either read from cover to cover or dip in and out of when you need some advice or inspiration.

Throughout each chapter there are several reflection points for you to use to help you consider your own thoughts and feelings on certain key points. These are designed not only to be a catalyst for thought, but also for you to write in your responses as you progress from chapter to chapter. As I mention in many places in this book, every school has its own individual context, so it's almost impossible to take an idea off the shelf and expect it to work in a different setting without some form of differentiation. Applying your own school and year group context whilst reading each chapter will ensure that you are thinking deeply about the implementation of these strategies in your own school building and with your own cohort of students.

Each chapter also contains a professional perspective from a current or former head of year, giving an authentic view from their own experience of how the theory plays out in the everyday role of a head of year. These professional perspectives are packed full of golden nuggets and invaluable advice from professionals on the front line. With over 100 years of collective pastoral experience between the 14 contributors and me, you are sure to be getting a broad and balanced range of knowledge and experiences to learn from.

Finally, each chapter also has a 'Next steps' section for you to take your learning further. It includes a 'Read' recommendation for you to read more about this topic, a 'Connect' suggestion for you to connect and communicate with people in your school about some of the key points raised in the chapter, and a 'Reflect' thinking point for you to process your own thoughts on something specific to you or your school.

Whether you are using this book for your own personal and professional development, or as part of a school-led professional development programme to help train others, I hope you take inspiration from the many ideas, thoughts and golden nuggets that this book holds. Pastoral care is one of the most amazing roles in education and our children deserve the best there is.

# 1

# The role of the head of year

---

## CHAPTER OVERVIEW

In this chapter we will look at:

- stepping up to your first leadership role and the variety the head of year role offers
- the multitude of roles you'll be tasked with when performing as a head of year
- why going down a pastoral route rather than a subject leader route is a great way to start your leadership career
- the challenge of juggling being a classroom teacher and a head of year.

---

## Stepping up to your first leadership role

Once you've been in the classroom for a few years, got your feet firmly under the table and begun to feel relatively comfortable in your role as a teacher, it's natural to want to start thinking about the potential of further responsibility within your school. In most schools, this usually takes the form of either a subject-based responsibility or a pastoral one. Subject responsibilities normally start with a department teaching and learning responsibility (TLR) or a second-in-department role, moving on to head of department, head of faculty or even director of subject in larger schools or multi-academy trusts. Pastoral leadership is normally centred around an assistant head of year role initially (particularly in bigger schools that require more pastoral leadership capacity) and then moving on towards head of year. So what should you expect if you take the head of year route?

## A role like no other

The role of head of year is certainly like no other in school. It is as rewarding as it is demanding and a pivotal role in the day-to-day turning of the cogs in a finely tuned and well-oiled educational machine. Pastoral staff in our schools are absolutely key to the safeguarding, welfare and wellbeing of our students, together with motivating and challenging them to do their academic best every day. Without these roles and amazing leaders, schools would not perform anywhere near as well as they do. The head of year is the perfect linchpin in school between pastoral wellbeing and academic achievement. In my view and many others, you can't have one without the other. The deep understanding that a head of year and their team have of every child is paramount to creating the right climate for success.

## On the front line

Of all the roles in school, apart from the main office and reception desk, the head of year is without doubt the most front line of all when it comes to dealing with parents, complaints and a whole raft of issues that come into schools every day of the week. It is this side of the job that is the most demanding and at times overwhelming, but it is also, in my opinion, the side of the job that gives the most satisfaction. Working closely with families to solve troubling issues, providing support and advice when things aren't going so well and giving up your time to help make someone a better person is exactly what drives and motivates pastoral staff. The evidence that you're making a difference to someone's life can be magnified so much more in this role, far more than a classroom teacher would ever see. From playground fights, child protection cases and family bereavements to sexual relationships and alcohol and drugs, you'll see it all if you stay in the head of year role long enough.

## *Every day is different*

Unlike a classroom teacher, there is no set timetable for how things will pan out every day when you become a head of year. This may sound concerning to those of us who like routine, but to the ones who like to think that every day might be different to the last, then the head of year role will certainly light your fire. When I was a head of year, I always used to go to work thinking, 'I wonder what I'll be dealing with today.' Whenever there was a knock at my office door and a student or a teacher came in saying, 'Have you got two minutes, Sir?', I always used to prepare myself for absolutely any eventuality. Many a time those allegedly two-minute conversations used to completely take over my day, clearing my diary of any other commitments and having to get cover for my lessons. But on other occasions, it might have just been a 30-second conversation, giving some advice or praise, leaving me the other 90 seconds to take a breath and feel relieved that it wasn't one of those other conversations.

As we explore in Chapter 14, page 225, your days will be significantly different depending on the year group that you are leading. Days at the start of the year in Year 7 may be taken up dealing with friendship issues and fallouts on the playground, whereas towards the end of the year in Year 11 significant time may be spent dealing with students knocking on your door who are struggling to cope with exam stress. However, all children in all schools are different. What happens at home the night before might significantly alter the way a student presents in school the next day and the mood they are in. Understanding the triggers to different behaviours and uncovering the catalysts behind certain situations is extremely interesting and imperative to being a successful head of year.

## Personal reflection

Why are you looking to go down the pastoral leadership route of progression in school, rather than the subject route? Is it out of passion or circumstances?

_____

_____

_____

_____

_____

What excites you about being one of the first points of contact with parents when it comes to the multitude of issues that a head of year has to deal with?

_____

_____

_____

_____

_____

# A multitude of roles

Growing up, you may have had grand ideas of being a doctor, nurse, policeman or lawyer. If that's true, then you've probably landed your dream role in becoming a head of year. Having done the role earlier in my career for nearly five years, I think I had to be every one of those professions almost daily to the students in my care. As I've mentioned, pastoral leadership will develop you personally and professionally like no other role can. When you initially train to be a teacher, you probably didn't think about becoming all of those people (and you probably weren't trained to be), but in the day-to-day role of a head of year, it is essential that you develop those skills fast.

Let's take a look at some of the roles that you will undoubtedly have to 'play' whilst leading your year group.

## *Judge and jury*

Students, teachers, parents and outside agencies will come to you with information about one of your students and expect you to hand out on-the-spot sanctions as harsh as corporal punishment. It is your job to listen to that information, put it into context with what you know about the student, their background and the situation, and then make an informed decision about what to do without jumping to immediate conclusions.

## *Prosecutor and defence lawyer*

From time to time you'll need to build up a case of what's happened, why it's happened and what you think should be done about it. This might be simply for a senior leader to help with an ongoing investigation about an incident in school, or it could be for something more serious like a permanent exclusion, or for social services in the case of a safeguarding investigation. Either way, it's vital to develop your skills in how to investigate an incident in a timely fashion, accurately recording the facts and preparing a coherent report ready to inform the next stage of the process.

## Doctor and nurse

There's never a day goes by in a big school where a student doesn't report to your office feeling sick. In the first instance, your kind, warm-hearted side wants to send them all home so they can be tucked up in bed, but before long you begin to use your experience to look behind the tears to find out what is really wrong. In no time at all, you'll become an expert in what type of symptoms require first aid or being sent home, as opposed to students who may be masking something else, or who just need to dry their eyes and get on with the day ahead.

## Police officer

As head of year, you are the sheriff for the children in your care. In some big schools, this can mean being responsible for the behaviour and conduct of up to 300 students. Law enforcement becomes your day-to-day role, along with the responsibility of ensuring that any sanctions handed out to students are in line with the crime. Sanctions that are too harsh will have you dealing with complaints from the offending student's parents; sanctions too lenient will have you fielding questions from the victim's parents, claiming that you have failed to do anything.

## *Counsellor*

At some stage or other, most students need to sit down and talk to someone. It may be an issue from home, a friendship problem in school, or just the stress that they are facing leading up to their exams. Either way, your skills and ability to just listen and be there for them should not be underestimated. You may be the only person they feel they can speak to about this issue, so it's vital that you provide the best support, advice and guidance that you can. Whenever you speak to students leaving school in Year 11, they almost always comment on how their head of year always made time for them when they needed it most.

## *Motivational speaker*

As the leader of the year group, it is your job to motivate your students to achieve the best they can. Student achievement is pivotal to success in all schools now and your senior leadership team will be relying on you to whip your students into shape so that they are performing at the top of their game. Regular battle cries, inspirational assemblies and motivational strategies are a key part of every head of year's toolbox.

## *Mediator*

Especially in the younger year groups in secondary school, you'll find most of your time is spent on mediating between students who have fallen out. 'She said this' and 'he did that' will be a familiar sound to any lower school head of year. This will certainly test your patience as a professional, especially when it feels like Groundhog Day every day, but spending quality time resolving the issues properly will save you hours of time having to go back over it in the future.

## *Mother and father*

Finally, without a doubt the most important of all the roles you'll play is to be a student's academic and pastoral mother or father throughout their time in your school. Parents are placing their precious child into your care and expecting you to do the very best you can for them. The more experienced you get in the role, the more situations you'll come across. Unfortunately, in some cases you'll need to be the very best parent you can be for them, because it's this that has been missing in their life.

Throughout the rest of the book, we'll explore these roles in more detail as we look at the various responsibility areas that fall within the day-to-day role of the head of year.

### Personal reflection

How many of the above roles do you feel you've already got the skills for?

_____

_____

_____

_____

Which roles do you feel you need to develop? How are you going to do this?

_____

_____

_____

_____

# Being a parent

Over the last few years there has been lots of talk about increased workload in schools, ultimately responsible for driving teachers out of the profession. There have also been some voices stating that you simply can't be a great teacher *and* a great parent due to the amount of marking, planning and preparation that you need to take home with you. Although I am fully supportive of reducing unnecessary workload, I don't believe this statement to be true. In fact, where a head of year is concerned, I believe that being a parent can make you even better at your job. Certainly in my own experience (and that of my wife, who was Head of Year 7 for nearly ten years), being a parent to two school-aged children made me a much better pastoral leader.

Now I'm not suggesting for one minute that having children is a pre-requisite for the role, or that you should go out and have a baby to enhance your pastoral CV, but anyone thinking about becoming a head of year who is already a parent shouldn't be put off. The empathy and understanding you'll have as a parent might just set you apart from the rest. I've been in many a challenging meeting with a parent when all I've had to say is 'I know how you feel, Mr and Mrs X. I'm a parent myself.' This immediately brings the situation down to reality, connects you with the parents on a human level and gives you the opportunity to break down any barriers or fears that the parents had about school. They are now just talking to another parent. I also feel that I've become a more mature and caring teacher since I've had my own children. My premise as a head of year was always that I needed to care for other people's children just as I'd care for my own – looking out for them, enforcing boundaries, rewarding them when they are great and being there for them when they need me.

# A great place to start

Now we've laid out the diverse nature of the head of year position and the different roles you'll have to take on, let's go back to the dilemma of whether to go down a pastoral route or a subject leader route when considering your first step up to leadership. As I've mentioned, I went down the pastoral route and I've seen so many others do the same in nearly 20 years of working in education. Interestingly, lots of teachers often think they'll set out to climb the subject responsibility route; however, I see more and more people every year become hugely interested in the pastoral route of responsibility. So why is this happening in our schools? It's certainly not because pastoral leadership jobs are seen as any easier than subject leadership roles. Ask most people in your current school and they'll probably tell you that their perception of the head of year role is that it is the hardest and most demanding job day to day of any in your school. Is it therefore because subject routes are already filled with staff who people perceive 'are not going anywhere anytime soon'? Or has the pastoral leadership role got so much more to offer in terms of personal and professional development?

## *Whole-school responsibility*

If your ultimate goal is senior leadership or headship, you'll need to gain some significant whole-school experience along the way. Although subject leadership is great, it can sometimes leave you concentrating on just your own area of the school and not the bigger picture. Having interviewed many people for senior leadership positions over the years, you can sometimes see the difference in understanding the bigger whole-school picture from an experienced head of year as opposed to a subject leader. The day-to-day involvement with rewards, behaviour, student data and dealing with parents across a whole year group can be quite significant in someone's professional development.

Many ambitious future school leaders see the head of year role as an essential stepping stone to whole-school senior leadership for this reason. In my own personal experience, I can only concur with this. Although when I became a head of year I didn't necessarily have a plan mapped out of where I wanted to go, it certainly provided me with all the skills and experience I needed to be a successful senior leader. Without the experiences that the role brought me every day, I don't think I'd be half the leader I am today. Certainly being awarded my first role as an assistant headteacher leading on behaviour, exclusions and child protection was all down to the experience I gained as a head of year. I don't believe that subject leadership would have prepared me in anywhere near as much detail as pastoral leadership did.

## *A new priority*

As a classroom teacher you'll be used to prioritising your teaching and having one single defined role in school and a set timetable that never changes, together with being in control of everything that's going on. The picture is very different when you are a head of year; suddenly you've got a new priority and it isn't your teaching. You'll soon come to realise that your priority now lies with the leadership of your year group, and your teaching unfortunately begins to take a back seat. The 'free periods' you once had to plan, mark or just recharge your batteries are now taken up dealing with a whole host of issues before you leave your office and run off to teach again.

Dealing with this transition of priorities can be very difficult for some teachers, especially if you are not prepared for it. You'll be constantly caught on the way to a lesson with that favourite line: 'Can I just talk to you for two minutes?', or interrupted mid flow in your lesson by a student who has been sent to you. In my own experience, and having coached others during this transition period from outstanding classroom teacher to head of year, what you need to ensure is that you have 'your shop in order' in your classroom. Resources need to be on hand, presentations ready and starter activities up your sleeve to ensure that even if you are a couple of minutes late because you've been stopped in the corridor, you can just turn up and perform as normal. This is a very different approach to what probably got you to this point in your career. Many of us pride ourselves on attention to detail, being in our classrooms before the students arrive, having resources and presentations already open on the whiteboard, and so on. It goes without saying that this will therefore take some time getting used to. I've met and worked with lots of teachers who, when they have become heads of year, have been so annoyed and disappointed in themselves that they feel they have let their own classroom performance slip. However, as long as you are prepared for this transition and don't get surprised or caught out by it, you'll soon come to love the role, the diversity and challenge it brings, together with the daily rewards you get for helping to shape the students in your care.

## Personal reflection

How confident are you that you can still perform to the highest levels in the classroom if your planning and delivery aren't your priority anymore?

_____

_____

_____

_____

_____

_____

_____

What structures, routines or resources do you need to put in place to ensure that your teaching delivery will not suffer as a result of taking on a new role?

_____

_____

_____

_____

_____

_____

_____

# Juggling two jobs

A particular challenge for new heads of years is the new element of juggling your new role with your continued role as a classroom teacher. Anna Wass outlines her experience when she took on her first head of year role.

# PROFESSIONAL PERSPECTIVE: READDRESSING THE BALANCE

### By Anna Wass, Head of Year at Acklam Grange School, Middlesbrough

As a classroom practitioner for five years before my role as pastoral lead, my remit was quite simple: ensure the academic achievement and progress of approximately 30 students within my classroom on a daily basis up to five times per day. I was extremely proud to be considered an 'outstanding' teacher, where experience, dedication and subject expertise collided over time to allow for the highest standards of teaching and learning. 'Free periods', or 'frees' as they were affectionately known, were a luxurious opportunity to grab refreshments whilst looking over students' work, share best practice with colleagues, prepare and plan fun and engaging lessons and even update myself on the latest educational methodology online that I might use with a particular group the following week. Looking back, it could be argued I was at the top of my game, maintaining that level of efficiency, delivery and teaching standard day after day, lesson after lesson.

In the earliest days of my career I had envisaged following the trajectory of the departmental or faculty route, but as time passed, it was clear that my passion was not the achievement of a child in a single subject area but rather the development of the student as a whole. Inevitably my career path moved into the pastoral sphere, being appointed a head of year. Overnight, the priority for me had changed; my responsibility for 30 students in a single subject had literally increased ten-fold. In all honesty I was not prepared for such a shift and the expectations that came with it. Where I was once delivering outstanding lessons, I quickly became disheartened that I was unable to maintain such high standards whilst spinning the plates of attendance, behaviour, welfare, safeguarding, a tutor team, SEND, LAC and EAL students, along with raising achievement in each and every child regardless of socio-economic background, ethnicity or family dynamic. The workload had become almost unbearable and overwhelming. Unfortunately, I was making sacrifices and it was the classroom that took the hit. I needed to readdress the balance.

As with many areas of education, efficiency is paramount and time management is key. As a head of year, time management and self-discipline have to become your professional best friends. The feeling that you must do everything is hard to shake but in order to be effective when your 'to do' list is expanding by the minute you need to:

1  Learn to be selective with your time and prioritise matters.
2  Be comfortable in verbalising the word 'no' to colleagues. As a head of year, the demands placed on you are already great, especially if you have a teaching timetable, and, should you agree or acquiesce to every request, you will burn out.
3  Be selective and ask yourself whether every commitment or task is essential. Is what you are doing feeding into and enhancing your overall objective?
4  Understand that part of pastoral leadership is knowing when to act and when to stand still.
5  Remember you are part of a team – you are not alone! Within your organisation you will have many staff who have more knowledge in certain areas than you and often more time than you.
6  Harness the strengths of other professionals around you and foster positive professional relationships. Working alongside others in a pleasant professional atmosphere maximises productivity and efficiency throughout the working day.

Ultimately, a good head of year will try to do everything. A great head of year will oversee that everything is done.

Establishing positive parental relationships early is highly recommended; meet them, talk to them, phone them and send positive texts and letters via the school's messaging systems. If your parents feel and know you have a genuine investment in their child's welfare and academic progress, you already lighten your workload. As the acting parent in school, the collaborative partnership between a head of year and the parent or carer at home serves as an invaluable method to facilitate positive outcomes.

## Personal reflection

How skilled are you with your own time management in school and your ability to prioritise your 'to do' list?

_____

_____

_____

_____

_____

What systems or tools might help you to master this?

_____

_____

_____

_____

_____

## Chapter 1 takeaway

### Key points

- Being a head of year is a demanding role, but comes with huge personal satisfaction in the knowledge you are making a difference to the lives of children every day.
- Every school day is different and you never know from one minute to the next what you are going to be dealing with when you get that knock on your office door.
- You'll suddenly be thrust into a multitude of roles every day to do everything from law enforcement to coaching and counselling.
- If you are already a parent, bringing your experience and parental empathy to the role can significantly improve your effectiveness as a head of year.
- Pastoral leadership provides a whole-school responsibility and an insight into the bigger picture of school improvement like no other middle leadership role offers.
- Your pastoral leadership responsibility overtakes your teaching on your list of priorities, but there are ways you can manage this.

### Next steps

- **Read**

  Read Stephen Drew's blog post on the Teacher Toolkit website titled 'Dear Parent, What I'd Really Like To Say…'. Stephen pinpoints what he'd really love to say to parents when they complain that we are 'picking on them', 'making it up' or that teachers are on a 'power trip'. This might give you some food for thought when dealing with irate parents who see no wrong in their offspring.
  Link: www.teachertoolkit.co.uk/2013/01/02/parents-2

- **Connect**

  Speak to a current head of year in your own school to get their perspective on the role. What are the challenges that they have faced? What adjustments have they had to make professionally to have the capacity to perform well as a leader and also still as a classroom teacher?

- **Reflect**

  Reflect on your own ability as a classroom teacher to take on such an additional responsibility. Take some time to use the personal reflection questions in this chapter to prompt your thinking. Ask yourself whether you are ready for such a role at this stage in your career.

# 2

# Your readiness for the role

---

## CHAPTER OVERVIEW

In this chapter we will look at:

- determining whether you are ready to be a head of year and whether this is the right career move for you
- the skills and experience you need to be successful in the role
- self-evaluation
- plugging your gaps.

---

## Are you ready?

Having read Chapter 1, which should have given you a greater understanding of the diverse nature of the head of year role, we can now begin to take a deeper look at your own readiness for such a position. The professional perspective from Anna Wass in Chapter 1 demonstrates how your day-to-day priorities change when you become a head of year and, more importantly, how you need to be professionally ready for this new phase in your career. Moving into a pastoral leadership role without being professionally ready and extremely competent in your regular classroom abilities can have a significantly negative impact on all areas of your performance. Taking on a new priority without the competence and capacity to do so can mean that both priorities (classroom teaching and pastoral leadership) suffer significantly.

Although you may have taken some time whilst reading Chapter 1 to reflect on your initial gut feeling about whether you are ready for a head of year role (via the personal reflection activities), it is important to see this as a significant step in your professional readiness. Taking the time to do this thoroughly, rather than just applying as a knee-jerk reaction to an advert you see, or in response to a situation at school that pushes you to want to move on, may prove to be time extremely well spent. I've lost count of the number of teachers I've spoken to who tell me that their classroom teaching had suffered in the first year as a result of taking on a new responsibility, or the teachers who thought that a middle leadership promotion would prove to offer a better work–life balance because they wouldn't be teaching a full timetable all week.

# A toolbox of skills

In Chapter 1, we explored a multitude of roles that you'll be expected to fulfil as a head of year. From judge and jury to doctor and nurse, the modern-day head of year has to have an extensive toolbox of skills to dip into when called upon. In the forthcoming chapters, we will discuss each one of the following areas that you need to be skilled in, but it is worth initially reflecting on your current proficiency and experience via the personal reflection activity at the end of the list.

## *Leading a team*

As a head of year you will need to lead your team of tutors to provide the very best level of pastoral care every day. If you're working in a large school, you may also have to manage an assistant head of year and possibly a non-teaching pastoral assistant. As teachers we were never trained to lead other staff but simply to teach children, so this may be a new experience for you.

## *Working with others*

Effective and successful heads of year very rarely work in isolation. There once was a time when pastoral care was their sole focus, but more recently there has been a significant shift towards student achievement. This requires an accurate and acute understanding of targets, student performance data and working with other teams in school to have a full overview of the academic and pastoral profile of each child in your care.

## *Setting standards*

As the figurehead of your year group, you need to be the one who is setting the standards and ensuring that students meet them. It goes without saying that this needs to be completely in line with your school policies and vision. However, it's one thing having these written down in a policy, but another thing to be constantly looking out for them and demanding them at all times.

## *Managing behaviour*

As a rule of thumb, if you struggle to deal with behaviour issues in your own classroom or find it difficult to gain respect from hard-to-reach or disengaged students, then you'll probably find this even more difficult on a larger scale. Being a head of year means you'll come into contact with these students on a far more regular basis and it is ultimately your job to try to turn them around. Effective behaviour-management skills are therefore essential.

## Rewarding students

Although one of the easier and more pleasant sides of the role, it still requires you to be innovative in the design and shape of your rewards. If you still believe that every student loves a merit mark, a 'well done' stamp in their book or a certificate in assembly, then you might need to take a 2020 reality check. Rewards need to be diverse, creative and innovative to reach and motivate all the different students in your year group.

## Attendance and punctuality

If you want students to learn, progress and achieve, they need to be in school. A successful head of year knows the importance of students being in school on time and uses attendance data just as effectively as they use behaviour and achievement data. If they're not in school, then they aren't learning. Working alongside your attendance team and education welfare officer is vital if you want to bring about change in some of your harder-to-reach families.

## Safeguarding

Although we all do our annual safeguarding training and review the updates on keeping children safe in school, it's a completely different ball game when you are ultimately responsible for a child's welfare. An in-depth knowledge of the systems around safeguarding is essential, but for most new heads of year your real experience comes when you're dealing with it and not just passing it on to someone else like you'd have done from your classroom.

## Closing the gap

Closing the gap is far more complex than just knowing who your pupil premium students are on your seating plan. Heads of year are required to have strategies for how they are closing the gaps between non-pupil premium students and pupil premium students, as well as boys and girls, SEN students, EAL students and so on. These gaps don't just close by accident, or by luck; they require careful and strategic consideration about how the performance of these students in all areas can improve.

## Outside agencies

Just as it's important to work with other teams in your school for the benefit of the students in your care, it's also vitally important to work with outside agencies. Building professional working relationships with outside agencies is extremely beneficial. Being able to pick up the phone and get the support that a student or family needs is sometimes the most important thing that you can do for someone. Like safeguarding, this experience comes in the role, but an understanding of the agencies that can work with children and what they offer is obviously a great starting point.

## Dealing with parents

One of the toughest and most demanding aspects of the role of a head of year can be dealing with parents. We must all remember that every student in your care is someone's baby. Parents can be supportive one minute and irate the next. Heads of year are the front line of the school and need to be extremely skilled in working with parents and understanding their issues and highly proficient in working with them to ensure that they feel their son or daughter is in safe hands in your school. If you've got no time for angry parents, or don't like being on the front line, then you might be looking for the wrong type of middle leadership role.

## *Record-keeping and organisation*

As a head of year you need to be extremely organised. The very nature of the diverse role you play and the number of issues that come at you every day makes it almost impossible not to be. Accurate record-keeping is an essential part of this. Notes from meetings, incidents and telephone calls need to be accurately logged within your school systems so that other teams can access this information when required. If you're not organised as a classroom teacher, in control of your own day, you'll certainly find it a shock to the system when other incidents and issues control what you are doing and when you are doing it.

## *Assemblies*

Heads of year are naturally required to plan and lead assemblies from time to time. Even though all teachers stand up and talk to classes of students every day, leading an assembly to a whole year group can be a very different experience altogether. Heads of year therefore need to be just as comfortable talking to large groups of students as they are talking to their own classes.

## *Specific year groups*

As a head of year, you'll probably get the opportunity to follow your year group through the school. This means they'll get older year on year, thus bringing with them different age-related issues. Some teachers are great with certain year groups but not with others. Heads of year need to be able to build strong positive relationships with students of all years and maintain these as their students grow up.

### Personal reflection

How many of the above skills do you feel proficient in?

_____

_____

_____

_____

_____

_____

Which skills do you feel you need more experience in? How are you going to get this?

_____

_____

_____

_____

_____

_____

# Identifying and understanding your gaps

## *Self-evaluation*

Using the personal reflection activities in Chapter 1 is a quick and easy start to get you thinking, but these reflection points should hopefully be the catalyst for a more extensive process of self-evaluation. Take time to be honest with yourself about how comfortable, knowledgeable and experienced you are in the roles that were described in Chapter 1. If these are going to be the core aspects of your new role, then you need to be proficient in most, if not all of them. However, you must not be too critical of yourself. As human beings (and certainly teachers) we are always the most critical of ourselves when we come to evaluating our own strengths and areas for development. As a head of year, you do not need to be a national leading expert in all of these areas, but instead professionally competent to deal with the type of issues that pastoral leadership throws up every day. There are also areas that you only learn from experience and that, no matter how much training you do, you'll only really learn from being on the job and in those situations.

Self-evaluation must therefore be realistic and accurate, but not set so aspirational that you feel you'll never be able to be successful. One of the best things to do in terms of where to set the bar is to speak to the current heads of year in your school. Ask them about the skills you require, the experience you need and what they still find difficult. By speaking to these middle leaders, you may find that you have very similar skillsets and the only thing that sets you apart is your lack of experience from not doing the job. As I mentioned previously, sometimes the only way to learn things in such a diverse role as head of year is to be thrown into the deep end. Support is always on hand in every school from experienced senior leaders. Just because you are leading a whole year group doesn't mean to say you're going to have to solve every problem on your own. You will find that lots of senior leaders in schools have been heads of year themselves, so can quickly and easily provide support to less experienced heads of year who are dealing with a complex situation for the first time.

## *Peer-evaluation*

Although performing a self-evaluation is critical to identifying and understanding your areas for development, it is always important to ask how other professionals view you. This can sometimes be hard to hear, but it is worth its weight in gold. Our opinion of ourselves can sometimes be very different to the opinion that others have of us. This can be because we doubt ourselves, have low confidence or are generally modest about our impact and influence; yet other times it can be due to an inflated self-confidence or an inaccurate barometer of what constitutes quality. Either way, having the courage to ask a trusted close circle of colleagues about your strengths and possible shortcomings can be one of the most important reflection activities you ever do.

It is always worth remembering that you may find some of the feedback from your peers to be a little different from your own perception of yourself and this can be disappointing. However, you must remember that if this is how your colleagues truly view you, then you need to take this on board. These people subconsciously observe you every day at work in some way or another, so their opinions are extremely important and probably quite accurate. It is no good thinking you are good at something if everyone around you has a very different opinion of your abilities.

## Personal reflection

How confident are you right now of conducting a peer-evaluation of your skills and experience as a potential head of year?

_____

_____

_____

_____

_____

Which people would you ask to complete this peer-evaluation? Will this list of people give you a realistic and accurate view of your ability to be a head of year? (It shouldn't just be a list of your best friends in education!)

_____

_____

_____

_____

_____

# Plugging your gaps

Once you have a true and accurate picture of your readiness for a head of year role from both your peer- and self-evaluation activities, you can now look at how to plug any gaps you may have identified. Every person reading this book will be slightly different and this is understandable. It is fine not to be the finished article right now. It may be that the majority of your gaps are purely down to a lack of opportunity or experience,

YOUR READINESS FOR THE ROLE

rather than it being a reflection of your own proficiency. Any gaps you have can be plugged in a range of different ways and, depending on your context, you may choose to use a range of the following methods. Some ways will be more appropriate for certain gaps and contexts than others.

## *Current colleagues*

Every school has either head of year positions or some other middle leadership roles that involve being in overall responsibility for the pastoral and academic welfare of the children in a year group or key stage. These are the people on the ground, doing the role that you want to do, so where better to start than speaking to these people about helping to plug your gaps? This sounds perfectly plausible until you realise how busy these people are. Suddenly asking them to give up time to help train you might not yield the response you want. A better and more effective way is to ask if you can shadow them at some stage when they are involved in activities related to a specific skill. This might be in parental meetings, looking at academic data for the whole year group or dealing with an exclusion. This can also be the perfect way to witness these skills in a real-life situation, rather than in a false context like a training session.

Once you have identified these colleagues, you then need to take the time to approach them and ask them whether they are willing to help upskill you. To do this, don't catch somebody in the corridor when they are running to a meeting or on the way to a class; make some time to sit down with them at a time that works for you both. This way you can talk about why you are doing this and how important it is for you professionally, therefore probably gaining a much better response.

## *Visiting other schools*

If you feel, for whatever reason, that you can't approach the current heads of year in your school, or you'd like to see this role in another context, you might want to consider visiting another school. Although this may seem like the perfect way to get experience away from your own school and a way not to show your deficiencies in experience or skillset to the people around you, it can have its negative sides. Firstly, you'll need time out of school to do this. The experience you're looking for probably doesn't come after the school day finishes. You're probably looking to shadow and learn from someone between the hours of 8.30 am and 3.30 pm. To achieve this, you'll need a supportive headteacher who is willing to let you out of school. Secondly, with the nature of the role, it's quite difficult to map out when certain experiences will happen; therefore it's extremely hard to plan a visit to another school where you'll see everything you want to. You might get lucky, but equally you might come back without the exposure to the things you went looking for. The best way to try to achieve this, if you are looking to visit another school, is to try to arrange a series of visits over a certain period of time. Your visits may also coincide with certain events like parents' evenings or assembly days. This way you'll hopefully get a far better insight into their role and the skills they use.

## *External courses*

If you haven't been able to gain the experience from one of the other approaches, you may feel that you need to look at a specific external professional development course. The primary benefit of this approach is that you get the chance to be away from school and have some quality time to truly learn and reflect on your own development. However, sometimes you can feel that some of the presenters are a little bit removed from the reality of school life and that you could get a better experience with somebody who is presently doing the head of year role in your own school.

## *Action plan*

Before you begin to embark on plugging your gaps via one or more of the above methods, it is sensible to sit down and plan out how and when this will all happen. A quick action plan document that has a list of every gap you are aiming to plug, followed by how you are going to do it and by when, means you're probably far more likely to stick to it. As teachers we're all extremely busy, so the chances are, in a couple of months' time, if you haven't committed your plan to paper, you will probably be too busy to remember what you were going to do. (Does this sound familiar?) Action plans also help you feel a sense of fulfilment when you tick things off that you have achieved and serve as a reminder of the goal you have set yourself.

# Is this the right career move for me?

Leaving the constant comfort of your familiar classroom for a promotion to head of year can be a daunting proposition. How do you know whether this is going to be the right career move for you at this stage of your career? Ryan Oates outlines his reasons why he knew that the time was right to move into pastoral leadership.

## PROFESSIONAL PERSPECTIVE: KNOWING WHEN THE TIME IS RIGHT

### By Ryan Oates, Achievement Team Leader at The St Lawrence Academy, Scunthorpe

I was a newly qualified teacher (NQT) when my school went through the transition of becoming an academy. Throughout this time, I remember feeling very excited about what opportunities lay ahead. When the role of an 'Achievement Team Leader' (head of year) was advertised, I felt nothing but delight over the prospect of applying. I loved the direction and vision for the new academy and I knew straight away that this would complement my qualities and be the perfect job (despite some concerns voiced from other staff that it may have come too early for me). Ten years later and the role continues to provide me with the opportunity to embrace my passion for helping students develop and grow into young adults who are fully prepared for life beyond their secondary education.

So why did I know I was ready for pastoral leadership? I firmly believed that the pastoral career pathway really suited my personality, skills and characteristics. A strong desire to nurture, help and support others has always been my moral purpose, hence the reason I became a teacher, and I have always approached all aspects of my job with a positive, enthusiastic outlook and a passionate belief that I can bring the best out of people. I therefore felt ready to take on the many roles that exist when leading a year group.

I had previously been encouraged to make significant contributions to the whole school by introducing new reward trips, delivering school assemblies, supporting the inclusion team and delivering activities in our local community. This gave me a taste of making a real difference within our learning community and left me desperately wanting to do more. I was well prepared for the challenge to develop new opportunities for students, remove barriers to learning and use my creative ideas to implement new pastoral strategies with a year group.

I had once visited some Year 7 students, in my role as a tutor, that were being educated off-site due to their challenging behaviour. The ability to build a good rapport with these students and their families eventually proved pivotal in helping the boys return to school and demonstrate a positive change in their attitude to learning. The daily belief that you can make an impact like this is essential to being a successful head of year.

Finally, I knew that I could dedicate the patience, enthusiasm and time needed to really shape the character and culture of my year group. I passionately wanted to be instrumental in providing a cohort of students with a fulfilling and successful journey through school, celebrating success and achievements, making special memories and enjoying treasured moments together. This was my vision and I was ready to share this with a team of tutors to make sure we made the difference to our young people.

In my experience, you will know that the time is right if:

- You have a desire to help students further than just in your own classroom.
- You can build strong relationships with students, parents and other teachers.
- You have a passion for removing barriers to learning.
- You feel you still have time and energy left at the end of the week to do more than just teach, whilst still maintaining a work–life balance.

## Personal reflection

How will your personality and individual characteristics enable you to shine in this type of middle leadership role?

_____

_____

_____

_____

_____

## Chapter 2 takeaway

### Key points

- Think about where you are in your career. Is this the right time for you to move on to becoming a head of year?
- The skillset that a head of year requires on a daily basis is vast and diverse. Have you got what it takes to be successful in this type of middle leadership role?
- Take the self-evaluation process seriously. Take time to figure out where your strengths and development points are.
- Prepare an action plan to address any areas of development you may have that might stop you from being an effective and successful head of year.

### Next steps

- **Read**

  Read _Bloomsbury CPD Library: Middle Leadership_ by Paul Ainsworth for a comprehensive guide on how to know if you're ready for middle leadership, the type of roles available and whether pastoral middle leadership is for you.

- **Connect**

  Widen your professional network outside of your own school by using social media sites like Twitter and LinkedIn to connect with likeminded professionals. This can also be a great way of being able to plug your gaps and receive help without broadcasting it to your current colleagues.

- **Reflect**

  Is this the right time in your career to make a move into middle leadership? Are there potential opportunities coming up in your own school? Or will you have to look externally for a head of year role?

# 3

# Applying for your first role

---

**CHAPTER OVERVIEW**

In this chapter we will look at:

- picking the right school
- the application form
- the letter of application
- preparing for interview
- interview tasks.

---

## Picking the right school

When thinking about moving into middle leadership as a head of year, it is worth taking some time to make sure you pick the right school to work in. A snap decision to apply for and get the first job you see might end up being a decision that you wish you hadn't taken. We all know the saying, 'the grass isn't always greener', and in education this can be even more amplified. Moving to a school that is under pressure from Ofsted, the local authority or a multi-academy trust takeover can, for some, be a pressure that takes its toll both mentally and physically.

For others, this is the motivation that gets them out of bed in the morning. You need to work out what's right for you.

## Current school

In my experience (from this happening to me and also seeing it happen at the schools I've worked in), the majority of head of year jobs are advertised internally. Putting an external advert out for a head of year could mean that they would receive applications from teachers in a number of different subject areas, most of which they might not require. Therefore, an internal advert means that the school can just offer a TLR that will add to someone's existing role.

## External applications

There are, however, some adverts that are advertised externally (I have seen this happen once in one of the schools I've worked in). In this instance a school may attach the head of year responsibility to an existing advert to see whether they can improve the quality of applicants for that subject post. For example, it might be an English job, but with the possibility of a head of year role for the right applicant. This way it gives the school the option of just appointing an English teacher, or appointing someone to teach English and be a head of year if they get the right person applying. However, these adverts are few and far between, so it's worth keeping your eyes open and your ears to the ground if you are looking for a change of school.

## Catchment area

Where you live may have a significant influence on where you want to be a head of year. Until now, you may have thought that living in the catchment area that you teach in might have been quite favourable, with short travelling time to and from school. However, when you become a head of year, you suddenly have far more dealings with some of the families in your local area than just teaching their son or daughter once or twice a week. This can be viewed as a positive or negative aspect and it all depends on your own personal preference. Is it more favourable to know the families you're working with, understand the catchment area and the issues it may have? Or do you feel that being responsible for the behaviour, child protection issues and general welfare of these students and their families is a little too close to home for comfort? Either way, it is worth taking the time to reflect on this so that you make the best decision possible when considering a move into middle leadership.

## Personal reflection

How comfortable would you be operating as a head of year in the same catchment area you live in?

_____

_____

_____

_____

_____

What would be the positives and negatives to this situation if you were given the opportunity?

_____

_____

_____

_____

_____

# Picking the right role

In today's schools, there are many different middle leadership roles that look after the pastoral welfare and academic performance of a cohort of students. With the growing diverse nature of how different schools are now organised, managed and led, this brings with it different staffing structures that aren't always mirrored in other schools. It is therefore imperative that you know what you are applying for and what your current skillset matches best.

## Assistant head of year

In larger schools, some staffing structures have assistant heads of year working under heads of year. This is the exact route that I took when I first moved into middle leadership. Working as an assistant head of year can be a superb opportunity for a less experienced teacher to begin their transition away from the classroom as their only priority and into pastoral leadership. These roles let you live and breathe the role of a head of year, but with someone there to guide you and help you grow professionally. As previously discussed, these roles are usually advertised internally in most schools and are well worth looking out for.

## Head of year

This is the traditional head of year role that we discussed in depth in Chapter 1, page 3. For schools that don't have assistant heads of year, the head of year is the all-encompassing pastoral and academic leader of a year group. Some staff move straight into this role as their first middle leadership position, whereas others cut their teeth as an assistant head of year first. This will all depend on your experience, the size of school that you work in and the opportunities that present themselves to you.

## *Key stage coordinator*

Some schools now have key stage coordinators who are responsible for a whole key stage, rather than just a single year group. Due to the size of these cohorts, this can be a far more challenging and diverse role than a traditional head of year and would potentially be a step too far if you have had no previous pastoral leadership experience. However, depending on the size of the school and the nature of the job description, you may find this quite appealing.

## *Student performance manager or achievement leader*

With schools now focussing on student performance data more than ever before, some schools have decided to move away from the more traditional head of year roles and create middle leadership positions focussing on student achievement. In these structures there is a clear emphasis on progress measures, data and student intervention programmes to ensure students meet their aspirational targets. The student performance manager or achievement leader will be not only responsible for pastoral welfare but held to account for the performance of their students in the classroom as well.

## Personal reflection

Do you feel you have the necessary experience and skills to take on a traditional head of year role right now, or do you think a midpoint step as an assistant head of year would be best at this stage of your career?

_____

_____

_____

_____

Have you got sufficient understanding of student performance data to take on a role that would require you to oversee pastoral care and academic achievement?

_____

_____

_____

_____

_____

# Applying for your first role

The application process will be different depending on whether the vacancy is for an internal role at your current school or an external role you are applying for at a different school. However, both should be taken as seriously and as professionally as each other. The last thing you want to do is to think that just because it is an internally advertised position, you don't need to show the very best of what you are capable of. Basic mistakes and a slapdash approach to the way you apply for a role could see you eliminated from the running immediately. I know from personal experience of looking at internal applications that if you receive one right at the last minute that has literally been thrown together because the applicant thinks they don't have to put too much effort into it, it immediately raises questions about how they'll conduct themselves in the role. If this is their 'A game', then what will they be like under pressure with a 'to do' list as long as their arm?

## *The application form*

This will usually only be required for external roles. If applying for an internal position, your current school shouldn't waste your time collecting basic information that they already have on you.

Application forms tend to be fairly standard items nowadays, but it is important not to overlook the importance of this part of the process. Even though most application forms look similar in their design, it is surprising how many people fall down at this stage because they have failed to answer specific questions correctly. Always remember that if it's on the form, then it's important. Take time to read the question and understand what it is asking you for before you begin. I'm sure you preach this approach to the students in your classes about examinations, but it's just as important to do it ourselves when we only have a few bits of paper to showcase our suitability for a role.

One of my personal pet hates is a handwritten application form. Even though you may like the look of your own handwriting, I have always felt that word-processed and typed application forms look far more professional. Feel free to draft and scribble your answers out on a printed application form to begin with, but then word-process your final version in the digital application form that the school will have no doubt provided you with.

## *Letter of application*

For internally advertised positions, this may be the only document that you have to submit. If you are applying externally, you may be asked to submit a letter of application as an addition to the basic application form. This should not be mistaken for an email that merely has the application form attached to it, or an email to your current headteacher simply stating that you want to be considered for the role. Crafting an unstructured letter is the first task to see whether you are literate and can write a professional letter home to parents in your year group.

A good letter of application should sell yourself and tell your story of who you are and why you want to be a head of year. The letter should also demonstrate your passion and commitment to education, including why you are specifically applying for the role at that school. Make sure it doesn't just look like a standard letter written for a number of jobs. Take time to include some information about the school so you can demonstrate that you have done your homework. This might just be the edge that you need to get a chance to showcase yourself at interview.

## *Basic mistakes*

Once you are confident that you have all the desired information in either your application form or your letter, get someone else to proofread them. It is a fact of life that our eyes only read what we think we have written. Trying to proofread your own work is virtually impossible because your eyes skip over the small typos and mistakes and focus on the key messages that you are trying to communicate. This is something else that we tell our students, but we need to remember to do it ourselves. It is surprising how many letters and application forms I read that contain so many mistakes.

# Preparing for interview

If your application documents hit the mark, then you'll be invited to interview. Between getting notification of your interview and the day itself, there's a lot of work to do. Simply thinking that you can just turn up in the interview room and talk the talk could be a costly mistake. Although you will have been through a teaching interview previously, you might have been in the same school since that time. Attending an internal interview for promotion, or being invited to an external interview, can be a tough experience.

## *Professional preparation*

Whatever your previous experience of interviews, it is unacceptable not to have done your homework on the school. With the amount of information publicly available on the internet, together with the information that the school will have sent you in terms of what they are looking for, being underprepared is simply not an option. Remember that although the school want to find out how good you are, they are also looking to see what you know about the school, how passionate you are about working there and whether you are the right person for the head of year role.

This is also a time to do some soul-searching and work out for yourself what your personal ethos for education is. You can be sure that the interview panel will want to ask you what you stand for, what you'll fight for and what you want for the students in your care. Think about what you'd say if you were talking to prospective parents at an open evening at your school or at your first Year 7 parents' evening. What would you say to those parents about how you'd care for their children and motivate them to become the best they can be?

## *Visiting the school*

If the role you are looking at is an internal vacancy in your current school, then you'll know all about your school already. However, if you are applying for an external role, you should seriously consider visiting the school prior to submitting your application form. There are two reasons for visiting a school prior to an application:

- to learn more about the school to see whether it is the right school for you

- to show your enthusiasm and to try to create a good first impression that will help put a face to a name for the shortlisting team.

Most schools will designate a few slots when you can visit. Some will be in the school day and some will be after school to cater for everyone's availability. In my experience I would strongly suggest asking your headteacher whether you can visit the school in school time so that you can truly experience what it is like. A building with no children in can be soulless and it can be difficult to gain a true picture of what the school is like.

When you visit the school, go around with your eyes truly wide open. Look at the standard of uniform, litter, wall displays and everything that can build up a picture of the school. Think about the staff you meet or bump into during your tour. What impression do they give you of the school and what it is like to work there? Go with a list of questions in your head that you might want answering.

Lastly, your visit is a perfect opportunity to gauge exactly how far away the school is from home. This becomes even better if your visit is around the bookends of the day so you can drive to the school in rush hour, gaining a more authentic feel for how long it would take you to travel there every day.

# Interview tasks

Although every school may conduct their interview day in different ways, the following are tasks that are regular features in either internal or external head of year interviews.

## *Telephone call*

A favourite on many interview panels that I've been on for pastoral leadership roles is a telephone call from an irate parent. The call is set up using a current member of staff as the parent and they are calling to complain about some aspect of the school. As the head of year on the front line, you need to manage these situations professionally, giving confidence to the parent that you'll deal with the situation, but, on the other hand, you won't just give in to their demands. Typical themes for this phone call are bullying, uniform or holiday requests. Your call will be listened to by members of the panel and everything you say will be considered in line with how the school would want to be viewed by parents. See Chapter 12, page 193, to help you navigate this if you feel you need to develop your ability to communicate effectively with parents.

## *In-tray task*

This is usually a simple task of prioritising jobs. You will normally be given a list of items that have landed on your desk and you need to prioritise them in order of how and when you will deal with them. Look out for any safeguarding issues that clearly need to be dealt with immediately. The other thing to note is that some schools will give you far more issues than you can physically deal with on your own. This is done on purpose to see whether you can use your delegation skills as a head of year and get your team of tutors to help you. This task is not about how you will personally resolve all the issues; it's about how you can ensure that all of the issues are resolved as efficiently as possible. See Chapter 4, page 62, if you'd like some more guidance on leading a team of form tutors ahead of the interview.

## Data task

With so much data to judge performance against, a school could pick any number of data sources for you to analyse. With the shift towards the achievement of the students in your year group and not just their pastoral care, the ability to show that you understand data is essential. Typically, you will be given a specific amount of time to make sense of some data, followed by a task that involves writing up a brief action plan or planning a presentation on what you would do next as the head of year responsible for this year group. This could be anything from attendance and punctuality to behaviour and exclusions, or progress and achievement. If you want to learn more about managing data before the interview, see Chapter 5, page 78.

## Student panel

The views of the students in any interview process are very important and shouldn't be underestimated. These are the people you are serving and they have a very sharp eye for quality. The panel is usually made up of the school council, with a range of year groups represented. The students will be looking to see whether you are here for them, or just for yourself. Treat the students with the utmost respect and be careful not to patronise them. They will know their stuff and won't want to be talked down to.

## *Formal interview*

The formal interview may be the only task you do, but it may also be the final piece of the jigsaw after any one or more of the previous tasks. The panel will be a mixture of senior leaders and the headteacher, who will want to know, from your own mouth, how you are going to take this year group forward, ensuring their pastoral welfare and producing record results at the end of Year 11. However, what people sometimes forget in interview is that the headteacher and the panel are looking for a person whom they can work with, not just a real-life version of the Ofsted framework. They need to see the real you. A smile and a touch of humour in the right places can go a long way to letting them get to know the real you behind the guard of a formal interview.

# Being successful at interview

Thinking that you are ready for a move into pastoral leadership is one thing, but being ready for the challenges that an interview process will bring is another. Chris Farman outlines his keys to success in the selection process.

### PROFESSIONAL PERSPECTIVE: INTERVIEW SUCCESS

**By Chris Farman, Head of Year at Nottingham High School**

I knew as an NQT the role I desired. I desperately wanted to take on the role of Head of Year 7 as I knew that it would be such a diverse and exciting role to be involved in. Transition from Year 6 to Year 7, open days and parent information evenings, academic monitoring, pastoral support, leading on PSHE, marketing the school... the list goes on.

Once I knew that my aim was to become a head of year, I collated a number of head of year job descriptions. Some, of course, differ from school to school, but many have similar responsibilities, such as utilising the school's sanction system to discipline appropriately, investigating bullying incidents, leading year group assemblies and so on. This provided me with a clear list of areas in which I needed to develop my experience and expertise. In developing these areas that I had identified, I shadowed the current Head of Year 7 in my school for a significant period of time. This gave me the opportunity to assist in dealing with incidents, planning and leading year group assemblies, and meeting with other heads of year to discuss the challenges they faced and the strategies they were currently leading on. All of these experiences were driven by considering and reflecting on what it takes to be an outstanding head of year and how I could demonstrate, via an application form and in an interview, that I could be the right person for the role.

By the time the Head of Year 7 vacancy was advertised, I was confident in believing I could be successful in the role. I genuinely felt that I'd put myself ahead of other candidates. The next step was to consider how I could take the year group forward and what strategies I wanted to implement during my time in the role. Having a clear vision is vital ahead of an interview, as it is important to demonstrate that you have the ability to make change happen. All too often, leaders talk a good game, but are unable to implement their plans in the stark reality of day-to-day school improvement. It is important to have taken the time to have thought about what your strategies for improvement will be before you step into the interview room.

The interview process can often be one of the most terrifying experiences of your professional career, particularly when applying for your first major leadership role, but it does not need to be. If you prepare meticulously and thoroughly, you will be in pole position to take your first steps into middle leadership. Here are my three keys to successfully preparing for an opportunity like this:

- Search the internet for head of year job descriptions and highlight what it takes to be successful in the role.
- Be proactive in gaining as much experience as possible before the vacancy you desire arises.
- Ensure that you have a vision for how you will develop the role to get the best out of the students in your care.

## Personal reflection

Search the internet for head of year job adverts and descriptions. What are the key themes that they are all looking for in a successful candidate?

_____

_____

_____

_____

_____

What would be your vision for getting the best out of the students in a year group you were appointed to?

_____

_____

_____

_____

_____

## Chapter 3 takeaway

### Key points

- Picking the right school to begin your middle leadership career in is extremely important. Whether you choose to progress in your own school or move to another school for your first pastoral leadership post, it is imperative to get that decision right.
- Pastoral leadership roles in schools across the country are all slightly different from each other, depending on the school structure. Make sure you take the time to understand the core role, what is expected from you and what skills are required. Have you got what it takes to be successful in whatever you think about applying for?
- The application and interview process is your opportunity to showcase the very best of you. Take each stage as seriously and professionally as the next. Do your homework on the school and the role. Take every opportunity to impress the shortlisting team and the panel with your desire to work at the school and be successful in that role.

### Next steps

- **Read**

  Read Chapters 5 and 6 in *Bloomsbury CPD Library: Middle Leadership* by Paul Ainsworth to get the very best tips on how to apply for your first middle leadership role and be successful at interview.

- **Connect**

  Speak to people in your school who have been successful in the interview process to become a head of year or who sit on interview panels of this nature. What was it like for those successful candidates? What did they have to do? And what does a panel member want to see from an applicant?

● **Reflect**

Are you looking to move schools in order to fulfil your ambition of becoming a head of year? If opportunities do not present themselves in your own school, are you prepared to move schools, even if it means significantly more travelling time each day?

# 4

# Leading and learning

---

## CHAPTER OVERVIEW

In this chapter we will look at:

- developing your pastoral leadership skills
- deliberate practice
- leading your team of tutors.

---

## Developing your pastoral leadership skills

After reading through the first three chapters, you'll hopefully have now been successful at interview and landed your first head of year job. However, being successful at interview is one thing, but being effective in that role is another thing altogether. Unfortunately, your initial teacher training route (if it's anything like the ones I've been involved in or had experience of) will probably not have given you any training whatsoever on leading people, managing others and stepping into a middle leadership role of responsibility. No matter how good you are as a classroom teacher, your new role will require a new set of skills in order for you to be effective. Pastoral leadership in the form of the head of year role has little to do with lesson planning, marking books or designing assessments and, like we discussed in Chapter 1, a lot more to do with investigating, mediating between and motivating the students in your year group.

If you used the advice in Chapter 3 to gain some experience prior to applying for your first role and you were able to shadow a current head of year, then you may already have a head start when it comes to developing your craft as a new pastoral leader. These experiences should have given you a great insight into the work that goes on behind headline performance tables and the type of skills you'll need in order to be an effective and successful head of year. However, don't be fooled or lured into thinking that just because you've shadowed someone for a few days, or have had experience of a difficult conversation, you've ticked it off your list and you're now a master at it. Every experienced head of year will tell you that all situations are different, every difficult conversation is unique, and you'll never be fully prepared and experienced to deal with everything that comes your way. This is the one job in education that can be a truly steep learning curve each and every day. I regularly have conversations with highly skilled and experienced heads of year who have been doing the job for years and tell me that they've just dealt with a completely new situation that they've never come across before.

Although new situations that you've never before encountered will regularly end up at the door to your pastoral office, it's important to understand that, even if the nature of the issue may be different and the content might be new, the way you deal with it and the skills you need to resolve it are always quite similar. It is your toolbox of pastoral leadership skills that you will constantly dip in and out of to help you resolve highly complex situations with the students and families you deal with. The more experiences that you encounter, the more you are able to draw on your breadth of skills from your toolbox to help you. The skills needed to diffuse an angry parent in reception or chair a tense meeting are the same, irrespective of the nature of the situation. However, this can be easily forgotten and can be intimidating for heads of year new to the role. The thought that you are walking into a situation you have not dealt with before can be a stressful one unless you remind yourself that you are taking your toolbox of pastoral leadership skills with you.

## *Deliberate practice*

Although previous experiences can count for a big chunk of your toolbox of skills, they don't always mean that you'll get better at something. If you keep doing the same thing in the same way, all that your experiences do is further cement any bad habits you have or create hard-wired responses to a set of circumstances. In order to change our practice, or seek to become better at something, we must change the way we do something. One of my favourite sayings is 'If we always do what we've always done, then we'll always get what we've always got' (attributed to Henry Ford). Therefore, developing your pastoral leadership skills requires a significant element of deliberate practice. For example, sitting in a series of parental meetings will undoubtedly give you experience at meeting with parents, but what element of these situations are you looking to become better at? Do you always end up on the back foot to begin with? Is this something that you want to get better at and stop from happening in the first place?

Deliberate practice requires you to think about a specific part of your role that you want to get better at and then study specific ways in which to do it better. This can come from physically watching someone do it better than you, reading or being trained on a new way to approach a situation, or just taking the time to personally reflect on a better way to deal with something that you're not completely happy with. Just like a golfer trying to fix an issue with his or her golf swing, there is probably something quite small that needs adjusting to make a big difference to the outcome. However, the golfer in question can head off to the golf course tomorrow to practise their swing. In education we can't just create these situations (and neither would we want to). Imagine wanting to get better at a certain part of resolving difficult conversations and purposefully creating a situation with a parent in order for you to trial your new techniques out!

In the education world, when training is invariably on the job and in live situations most days, deliberate practice requires you to do the following things:

- Reflect on the area of your practice that you want to develop or improve.

- Research what would constitute outstanding practice or alternative methods to bring about a better outcome.

- Wait for an opportunity to deliberately put into practice this new method or tweak to your current practice.

- Deliberately and consciously think about using the new technique or strategy throughout the situation or event; don't just use your autopilot settings.

- Reflect on whether the outcome changed, based on your deliberate change of strategy or technique.

It is, however, worth remembering that not every change you make will bring about an improved outcome and that doesn't mean that the change did not work. In some situations, no matter what you do, you may not be able to change or positively influence the outcome. This does not mean that you should immediately dismiss the new strategy or technique that you used by considering it a failure. If you believe in what you've researched, then try it again. You may just find that it works wonderfully well in a different context with a different situation. An experienced head of year will know when to use the right strategy or technique in the right situation.

### Personal reflection

Which areas of pastoral leadership do you feel that you need to deliberately practise in order to improve a certain outcome? Try to be as specific as possible in your thinking and reflect on one thing that you can deliberately change.

_____

_____

_____

_____

_____

How are you going to change these areas of your pastoral leadership and what will this look like in practice? What does the research suggest that you do? What have you seen others do that you feel will bring about a better outcome?

_____

_____

_____

_____

_____

# Leading your team of tutors

Being a tutor is an essential part of most classroom-based teachers' roles; however, if you asked everyone privately, it's probably not at the top of their priority list. This creates a challenge for every head of year – how do I get my team of tutors to play an active part of the pastoral care system every day and not just be a register-taker? Think back to either your own experience at school or the experiences that you've gathered since being in teaching – there is a significant difference between a tutor who just sees their job as taking the register in the morning and someone who values their role in caring for their tutees, motivating them and monitoring their individual levels of effort, behaviour and attainment, whilst managing to keep communication lines open with their parents. We've probably all been in schools where the consistency of experience for students at form time can be quite different.

As we know from any sports team or organisation, a team doesn't just pull together and work effectively automatically; it takes careful and deliberate leadership from the people at the helm. As the head of year leading your own team of tutors in school, you will need to consider the following areas to ensure that you lead your team in the most effective way possible.

## *Vision*

In order to get any collective group of people working towards the same goal, you need to share that goal with them. In this case, your ability to communicate your vision on the following two areas is essential:

- why you believe that the role of the tutor is fundamental to the way your school develops every student to achieve the very best that they can

- how your team and each individual tutor will play their part in achieving this.

Having a clear vision is great, but it's never going to be effective if it's only in your head. Taking the time to explain to your team how important their role is and how you'd like them to do it is the first essential step in leading your team.

## *Personal ethos*

Talking to your team (either as a team or as individuals) about your ethos for the pastoral care of your students can help to get people on board quickly. When you look at most high-performing organisations, you'll generally find that people work better for managers they believe in. Think of your own experiences. You are probably far more likely to run through a brick wall for someone with whom you share beliefs about education, rather than someone you feel is just doing something because they think Ofsted want to see it. By sharing your ethos and beliefs about pastoral care, it can help people understand your motives and see that they are all about the children in your care and not just about policies and external accountability.

## *Communication*

One of the hardest parts of leading your team is constantly keeping them in the loop about what is going on. With the pace with which things can happen in a pastoral office, you can suddenly find yourself swamped in a multitude of situations that need resolving quickly. The tendency can be to move from one situation to the other, forgetting to inform the relevant chain of people as you resolve each situation. Having experienced this as a tutor myself in my early days of teaching, it can be extremely frustrating to be told that you are all an essential part of the team and then not given any information when a student in your tutor group is excluded, only finding out when their parent rings you, asking for an explanation. Although communicating with your tutors when incidents happen takes extra time and adds another chain to the process, it is imperative if you really do see them as an essential part of your pastoral care team. You'll find that by communicating more regularly with them about incidents and issues that arise with members of their tutor group, they'll get more involved as a result, thus creating extra capacity in your team and reducing the need for you to feel that you have to do everything yourself.

## *Presence*

One thing that everyone has respected in every team I've ever been part of is a significant level of presence from the people leading that team. Whether it's because they want to see you muck in with everyone else or they want you to physically show them what your vision looks like, you can't underestimate what presence does for your reputation as a leader. There will of course be times when you'll need your office door shut and you have to learn to say 'no' (see the professional perspective by Anna Wass in Chapter 1, page 16), but if you're known as just an office manager because you're rarely seen on the front line, then people will quickly resent you for delivering orders without wanting to get your own hands dirty. My advice to increase your presence overnight is to:

- regularly visit tutor groups during registration time
- help out on the late gate whenever possible
- get out and about on the school yard and dining hall during breaks and lunchtime, taking the time to talk to both students and staff.

However, with the demands on the head of year office at these specific times (tutor time, breaks and lunchtime), this can sometimes feel quite difficult, if not impossible, to achieve. This is where you need to be disciplined to use your team effectively and your time wisely. If it's important to get around your tutor groups in the morning, then you'll make it happen. Having an assistant head of year can make this much easier to achieve, but even as a sole head of year there are ways to block off certain mornings for such activities unless an emergency situation presents itself.

## *Team culture*

Think of any team that you've ever been part of and reflect on what made it special, or why you wanted to join it or stay with it. Was it having a shared common goal? Was it the celebrating that came with achieving your common goals? Or was it the camaraderie and mutual trust that came with spending time together and working towards that goal? Whatever it was, you need to try to bring that to your team of tutors. How can you make your tutor team feel like a proper team and not just a group of people who have been asked to do something that they don't want to do? Depending on the nature of your team, the context of your school and the staffing profile in your team of tutors, this will need to be a bespoke solution. Some people will value certain parts of teamwork more than others, but it's your job as the leader to get the very best out of everyone, just as it was the manager of the team you first reflected on in this paragraph. Simple things like an end-of-term get together in a classroom for 30 minutes where you bring some crisps, cake and pop can be the little thing that brings people together.

## *Sharing outcomes*

A lot of the time outcomes of the pastoral leadership system can be seen by the leaders but not shared with the foot soldiers. How do your team know that they are doing a good job? How do they know that they are achieving the vision that you laid out for them? As you'll know only too well by now, there are so many performance indicators in school to tell you how well you are doing and what impact your strategies are having on your students. Taking time to share these key performance indicators with your team can help to close the loop on your vision – you've told them what you want them to do, you've told them how you want them to do it, so why not tell them how well they're doing it? Presenting some figures on improved attendance and punctuality, or a reduction in behaviour points or exclusions, could be just the tonic they need at the end of a long term when their responsibility as a tutor is gradually slipping down their list of priorities.

### Personal reflection

Reflect on what makes being part of a team so much more rewarding than working or performing on your own.

_____

_____

_____

_____

_____

How can you bring these elements to your team of tutors in order to improve pastoral care under your guidance?

_____

_____

_____

_____

_____

# Hitting the ground running

Hitting the ground running as a new head of year is imperative. You'll seldom be afforded breathing space and bedding-in time by the students in your year group. When the starting pistol is fired on the first day of September, it's all go from then on in. Steve Hoey reflects on how he was able to bring his team together to carry out his vision for pastoral care.

## PROFESSIONAL PERSPECTIVE: LEADING A NEW TEAM

### By Steve Hoey, former pastoral leader in secondary schools in Northamptonshire, Hull and North Lincolnshire

When I first became a head of year I was responsible for a team of 12 tutors and over 330 students. I was a relatively young and inexperienced leader who was in charge of a team of very different tutors, ranging from NQTs to some very experienced staff. I began by asking the students themselves what they wanted from their tutor. They told me that they wanted someone who was 'welcoming, strict, helped them with problems, knew their names, was polite, gave them confidence and supported them'. This helped shape the vision for my team. I wanted my tutors to build positive relationships with all the students in their tutor group and to consistently model behaviour that promotes respect, responsibility and resilience.

Developing a team spirit means fully involving the tutors and listening to them. The power of active listening and developing coaching skills to enable you to get the best out of your tutor team is so important. I only used to get one team meeting every half term, so I had to find other ways to build these relationships and allow the team to have an input into my pastoral vision. Clear communication was always the key. In a time before continuous email, I had to walk around and actually speak to the tutors. Today, I would suggest that this is still very important, but to ease the burden you can quite easily set up an email group; however, it's important to keep any messages to a minimum and businesslike. A weekly email update has always helped me to keep my team in the loop of what is going on.

Developing a year group identity is not just something done in assemblies but needs to be worked on every single day. I always saw tutor time as the key time – whether in the morning or at any time of the day. These ten to 20 minutes were so important, not only for giving out messages and checking that the students were all okay, but also for developing an ethos of co-operation and a sense of identity. I used to try to be strategic and cover one of the tutor periods every week. This gave the tutor a break and also allowed me to quality-assure what was going on. I did this on a rolling basis, so every tutor group was seen during a term.

Caring and nurturing is essential but with the best will in the world you cannot know every student in your year group, so you need to make sure that your tutors know every student in their tutor group. I would have an expectation that each tutor had regular contact with home, that they took the time to know each child and what they did outside of school, and that simple things like birthdays were celebrated. There are always 'camouflage kids' in every tutor group who, because they never raise their heads, go relatively unnoticed.

My top tips on leading your team of tutors are:

- Use the experience of your team and involve them in ideas and plans where possible. You will have a range of experiences and skillsets to help you.
- Celebrate your tutors. Share good practice amongst your team and build upon their strengths.
- Set up a buddy system for inexperienced tutors and NQTs.
- Involve your tutors in delivering assemblies, running seasonal events and charities. Give them enough opportunities to be fully involved.
- When building proactive relationships with parents and carers, don't wait until it goes wrong. Ensure that your tutors reach out and engage with parents in building positive home–school relationships. Positive phone calls home on Fridays can be brilliant in this respect.
- The hardest thing to do is leave your role at school. Try not to take it home. Have strategies in place to support you. Remember you cannot pour from an empty cup and self-care is so important.

## Personal reflection

What experience have you got from outside of education in leading or managing a team that you can apply to leading a team of tutors for the first time?

_____

_____

_____

_____

_____

## Chapter 4 takeaway

### Key points

- Whether you are an experienced head of year or new to the post, it is always good to have the mindset that you can keep learning. By seeking opportunities to learn from others and then using deliberate practice to develop your pastoral leadership skills, you will be constantly refining and improving your day-to-day leadership skills.
- It's important to take the time to develop your own vision for pastoral care under your leadership. You may have been used to doing things in isolation as a classroom teacher, but your focus now needs to shift to how you are going to motivate and lead others to carry out this vision.
- Once you have developed your vision for how you want your team to carry out pastoral care under your leadership, it is essential that you communicate this with your team. Regular communication in a range of ways helps you not only to monitor and support your team, but also to keep them up to speed with how they are doing in relation to raising achievement and whole-school improvement.

# Next steps

● **Read**

Read *100 Ideas for Secondary Teachers: Tutor Time* by Molly Potter. Here you will find a wealth of resources and ideas for your busy team of tutors and it will inspire form time ideas that are constructive and exciting, yet take little preparation.

● **Connect**

Speak to current heads of year in your school, or colleagues you know in other schools who are in pastoral leadership positions. What challenges are they facing in trying to lead their team of tutors to raise achievement in their year group?

● **Reflect**

Reflect on your own experience of being a tutor and part of a tutor team. What things made that team a good team to be part of and what things frustrated you?

# 5

# Raising achievement

---

## CHAPTER OVERVIEW

In this chapter we will look at:

- working with others
- student performance data
- school improvement.

---

## Working with others

To the outside world, raising achievement in an individual student may seem quite a simple process – get them to do better in their final examinations. However, as I'm sure you'll be well aware by now, it can be far more complex than this. In my own experience of being a head of year and having been a senior leader for over 15 years, it is very rarely the case that a student's examination success can be attributed to one factor, or one isolated input from a teacher. Raising achievement in any student or cohort of students, if done properly and effectively, is usually a team effort. Different teams or individuals within school have to work together, communicate and collaborate so that the end result is improved academic performance. Although this may sound easy and obvious, in the fast-paced reality of schools, it's not always that simple. Speak to anyone involved in sports coaching or team management and they'll tell you that the foundations for making a team perform successfully are built on having a clear and common goal that everyone is working towards. The problem we face in school is that, unlike a sports team whose goal is to win the game this weekend, most of the different teams in school have their own mini goals that they are being held to account for. Once you factor in the issue that some of these mini team goals are not conducive to another team's goals, you begin to see how complex this process can be.

## *The linchpin*

An effective head of year is the linchpin that holds everything together and can see cohesiveness to a raising achievement plan for each and every one of their students. This is not easy though and it requires you to see the bigger picture of school improvement as well as the fine details and individual needs of each student. There will undoubtedly be times when tough decisions need to be made for the benefit of either the school or the individual student, and you may have to fight for your students from time to time. This is where knowing your students and their individual needs becomes paramount. You are there to oversee the pastoral care and welfare of your students whilst helping them achieve the very best academic results possible. Without the care and attention that the traditional head of year provides, your students will simply become a number and a name on a spreadsheet – pawns in the data-driven world of continuous school improvement.

Let's look at a few examples of why some teams might be pulling apart when it comes to raising achievement, rather than pulling together for the benefit of the individual student.

## Individual subject team

Every individual subject leader or head of faculty is primarily focussed on their own mini goal – to raise achievement in their subject. Naturally this will be a more inwardly looking approach, based on their own subject priorities, and can from time to time cause you quite a few issues. What happens when two subjects want one of your students back for extra study or intervention on the same night? What do you do when a student comes to you stressed because they have two big subject deadlines to hit on the same day?

## Behaviour team

Throughout the year, your behaviour team should be there to support you and help you deliver high standards of behaviour in and out of the classroom. However, the focus on high standards of behaviour is not always in line with the focus on academic achievement. Take for instance a group of Year 11 students who have clearly and significantly flaunted the school rules and are speaking to staff in a disrespectful manner. Your gut instinct, along with the wishes of the behaviour team, is to remove these students from lessons and place them in your behaviour or inclusion area for a period of time. However, you then have individual subject leaders and senior leaders banging down your door telling you that it's vital that these students are in lessons because of the work that they'll miss in Year 11. The decision is then a critical one: do you give in to the academic demands of the school and risk the students thinking that they are untouchable in Year 11, or do you hold firm to your high standards? Either way, this decision needs to be taken with representatives of the wider school leadership team and in the best interests of everyone, not just the interested party who shouts the loudest.

## Attendance team

From time to time, students will be removed from mainstream lessons due to poor behaviour. Some students will not like this and will vote with their feet and stay off school, thinking that the punishment will just go away or be forgotten about. However, a strong behaviour team will not buckle and will usually just reinstate the punishment when the student returns. The problem arises when the student and the family say they are not returning if they are not going back into normal timetabled lessons. This is when the attendance team become concerned because, day by day, their attendance figures are dropping. A conversation then normally takes place between the education welfare officer and the behaviour team to ask whether the punishment can be dropped, so as to get the student back into school. This can be met with animosity from the behaviour team because they quite rightly feel that if they 'give in', then the same will happen next time and the student and their family will be able to call the shots. As head of year, if you're not already part of the conversation, you'll probably be brought into the situation at this point and be asked to make a decision on how to resolve this.

## PE department

Extracurricular activities are superb for the personal development of our students, but should this be an earned privilege or an unconditional right? What happens if a student is the captain of the football team but has been behaving poorly in school? Should that student be allowed to play for the team tonight? Your initial reaction might be no, but you might need to stop and think about the impact it will have on the rest of the team, who have done nothing wrong. Should the player be allowed to effectively 'get away' with their poor behaviour and still get the reward of representing the school, or is representing your school an earned privilege? This will require careful thought about that individual student because they will be representing the school in a public forum. You need to balance out the potential damage of other students and families seeing this student still representing the school knowing what has happened, together with the fact that this sport might be the only bargaining tool you have with that student. Telling your head of PE that you've made a decision that the captain of their team is not allowed to play probably isn't going to go down that well in the first instance without a full explanation of the bigger picture.

## Personal reflection

Take one of the scenarios from above and reflect on how you would solve this situation, using your leadership skills to ensure that all parties understand your decision and that the best interests of the student are at the heart of your decision-making process.

_____

_____

_____

_____

_____

How might you stop this scenario from getting to this point in the future or repeating itself?

_____

_____

_____

_____

_____

# Student performance data

With schools becoming increasingly reliant on student performance data to judge their effectiveness in a number of different areas, it is essential that, as a head of year, you understand your data. Without this understanding of all the different data that is collected and processed on your students, how will you know how well your year group are doing compared to your targets? It might have been sufficient 20 years ago to suggest that the year group are doing well because there hadn't been a fight on the school yard in the last week, but things have significantly changed since then. Today's school leaders (at both middle and senior level) are required to know not only about all the different types of student performance data, but also how to interpret it and use it to raise achievement. A good head of year can act on data that is given to them; a great head of year can use data in their daily role to identify an issue and put a strategy in place to resolve it before it becomes a significant whole-school issue.

Here are some examples of student performance data that you'll be expected to use in order to raise the achievement of a single student, or a cohort of students, in your care.

## *Attendance and punctuality*

High attendance plays a crucial role in raising achievement. Put simply, if students are not in school, then they are missing out on crucial learning. Getting them in the building on time is paramount if you want them to achieve their true potential. A Department for Education report into attendance in 2016 found that, in general, the higher the overall absence rate, the lower the likely level of attainment. Students with no absence are 2.2 times more likely to achieve five or more GCSEs at A*–C or equivalent and 2.8 times more likely to achieve five or more GCSEs at A*–C or equivalent including English and mathematics than students missing 15 to 20 per cent of Key Stage 4 lessons. Patterns of attendance or absence can also signal certain things. Is there an issue with a certain subject that a student is trying to avoid? As a head of year, you'll need to work closely with the attendance team to analyse your own year group attendance statistics. Attendance data is also worth exploring when dealing with an individual underperforming student. One of the first things that an experienced head of year will look at in this case is their attendance. Have they been in the building enough to be learning and progressing at the same rate as other students?

Understanding the context of this data is crucial. Is attendance in line with national figures or school targets? (Check the annual statistics published by the Department for Education for the latest national performance data.) And what does your analysis of attendance and punctuality data actually mean? Without reference to and knowledge of local and national norms, your data is pretty useless. One of your first ports of call will be to ascertain what the school targets are (and why they have been set like this in comparison to national figures), so that you can judge how well you are actually doing. This is important for explaining the impact of attendance to parents as well. Historically we've all been used to thinking that 90 per cent is a pretty good score to achieve in any test that we've taken since infant school. However, an attendance figure of only 90 per cent will significantly hold a student back from achieving. When you spell it out to a parent that 90 per cent attendance means that their son or daughter is having a day off every two weeks for the entirety of their school life, they begin to understand the significance of it.

## *Effort*

A key indicator of how well students will achieve is the level of effort that they are putting into each of their subjects. In most schools, this is now being collected as regularly as raw academic achievement data because it tells the story behind the grades. You can't do anything to fix a problem until you know why the problem is happening in the first place. A student who is struggling to achieve but putting maximum effort in will require a very different support strategy than a student who is not putting any effort in. An effective head of year will come to rely on these effort grades to see a true reflection of how students are applying themselves in classrooms across the school and where extra motivation is required, whether it be for a whole year group, small groups or individual students.

Knowing how to solve issues where low effort is being applied is a key part of the role. As head of year, you may be the only one with a clear overview of everything going on in that student's life and might be able to explain a sudden drop in effort based on something that is happening. It's your role to work with others to potentially find out what the root cause is and then communicate it to the rest of the teachers and professionals working with that student.

## *Behaviour*

Behaviour data can be quite vast and diverse. It can range from external exclusions figures to individual behaviour points in the classroom. However, it is absolutely vital that you understand it and regularly analyse it. Unlike other datasets that are inputted by teachers at predetermined points throughout the year, behaviour data (like attendance and punctuality) is live and ever changing. This is something that you need to keep your analytical eye on constantly so that you can see where problems are arising that are impacting upon academic achievement.

Behaviour points given out by classroom teachers is a perfect example of understanding the data before you act on it. One teacher might be giving extremely high numbers of behaviour points out and another may be giving none at all. The naked eye will automatically judge which teacher is struggling and which teacher (in some eyes) is therefore the better classroom practitioner. However, you might find that the teacher who isn't registering any behaviour points is actually letting the whole team down because they are letting students get away with poor behaviour and therefore masking where the real issues of underperformance really are. The teacher with high numbers of points may just be the only one using the system consistently.

Exclusion figures are also interesting to keep an eye on. Going back to what we discussed on page 74, some mini team goals do not help other teams within the same school. Exclusions are a prime example of this. When a student is excluded, they will automatically lose at least a day's attendance, meaning that this outcome might suit the behaviour team but not the attendance team. Critically, it's the job of the head of year to oversee, or at least be part of, all these decisions, because they are the one professional who has a full overview of the whole child.

## *Achievement*

In today's schools you can't turn around without seeing or hearing about the next data drop or deadline for inputting data. In order to track progress and intervene at accurate times, schools require data on student achievement to be regularly entered by teachers throughout the academic year. There is, however, a significant difference between how some schools want teachers to input data, and it's extremely important that you know what your school does and why they do it. The big difference is usually between current and predicted levels of achievement. Asking a teacher to input a current grade or level is very different to asking them to input a predicted grade or level. It's therefore imperative to understand the difference and to understand what that data is telling you about your students.

Depending on the school you work in, you may find you use one type of data or both.

As we discussed in Chapter 3, page 41, heads of year now occupy different types of roles. The more traditional head of year role would not have been too focussed on achievement data, and instead would have concentrated more on attendance and behaviour data. However, with the landscape shifting away from heads of year providing purely pastoral care and more towards heads of year being 'student performance managers', you can see why knowledge and understanding of this type of data are crucial if you want to play your part in raising achievement.

## Personal reflection

Do you know the national average for attendance last year? How does this compare to either your year group or a selected year group in your school?

_____

_____

_____

_____

_____

How many days were lost to exclusions last year in your year group or a selected year group in your school? How does this compare to national averages?

_____

_____

_____

_____

_____

By looking at either your year group or a selected year group in your school, how would you know whether they are currently on track to perform in line with school targets or national averages? What is your evidence?

_____

_____

_____

_____

_____

# The bigger picture of school improvement

As you move through your career and into middle and senior leadership positions, you begin to see and understand the bigger picture of school improvement. At first, it's all about your own class, your subject and your targets. But with experience comes understanding of the bigger picture and how you fit into that picture. In every school I've worked in, heads of year play a key part in the process of raising achievement every year. Their in-depth knowledge of every child and what is going on helps and influences others to make the right decisions that are mutually beneficial to both the student and the school.

Being a head of year also gives you a privileged position to be truly involved in the bigger picture of school improvement. It is a role that cuts across all areas of school, unlike other middle leadership roles such as subject leader or head of faculty. By the very nature of the role, you get first-hand experience of attendance, behaviour and achievement all together, giving you a much more balanced view of the sub-areas that need to improve in order for headline results to improve. Understanding that some school priorities naturally pull against others is extremely important (as we've already discussed on page 74). There will be times when you'll have to accept that you can't get your own way when making tough decisions because of the bigger picture. This doesn't mean that you've been superseded or that someone has pulled rank on you; it simply means that you've had to understand that school improvement is multi-faceted and that not everything we do complements another area of the school.

As mentioned in Chapter 1, page 12, this has huge benefits for your future career progression. Getting an early understanding of whole-school improvement is a fantastic opportunity and, in my own experience, can sometimes put you above subject leaders when it comes to applying for senior leadership positions. As a new head of year, my advice would be to get to grips with whole-school improvement as quickly as you can and take every opportunity to see how your decisions and actions fit into the bigger picture. Once you begin to understand and appreciate this, your decision-making process will become even stronger, as you will have a firm evidence base behind your reasons for making some tough and often unpopular decisions.

# Every child matters

Tom Smith reflects on how he's been able to support whole-school improvement and raising achievement of the cohort of students in his care, whilst also ensuring that traditional pastoral care and support is not overlooked.

## PROFESSIONAL PERSPECTIVE: RAISING ACHIEVEMENT, ONE STUDENT AT A TIME

### By Tom Smith, Head of Standards at Holy Trinity School, Barnsley

Raising achievement amongst a cohort of students is as multi-faceted as the most intricately cut diamond. Many different factors affect why a student achieves well or doesn't achieve well when they open their envelope on GCSE results day. As a head of year for six years, I have taken a year group through the whole process from Year 7 to Year 11 and watched on as they all opened their envelopes, feeling just as nervous, or maybe even more so, as many of the students in front of me.

Raising achievement is the same for everyone; however, depending on your setting, the realities of it are as varied as the students we teach. Therefore, rather than providing details of specific strategies, I feel it would be more appropriate to highlight three general traits that have helped me in the pursuit of high levels of achievement.

## 1. Relentlessness

- The pursuit of achievement never stops. There is not a period where you can take your foot off the gas and there won't be any occasions where you can relax, thinking that you have cracked it. Raising achievement is about marginal gains with your students: small pockets of students making small improvements all the time, leading to a widespread increase in achievement.
- Many different ingredients need to come together to enable widespread achievement – behaviour, attendance and engagement being a few. These are things that a head of year must chase constantly. Having a solid foundation

for class teachers to build upon will have the most impact out of anything.

## 2. Relationships

- It is no secret that relationships are important with your students; however, the relationships you have with the teaching staff, your students' parents and carers, and your senior leadership team are equally as important. Without support or 'buy in' from all the key stakeholders, the job is much more difficult.
- Developing trust with your students is vital. There will be occasions where your students don't necessarily agree with what you are asking them to do, but if they trust you then that will go a long way to achieving the outcome you want. Students, parents and other staff *must* trust you and have faith that the decisions you make are the right ones for the situation, the student or the school.

## 3. Resilience

- The ability to get back up when you've been knocked down, to carry on despite numerous setbacks, is something that you can develop. The growth mindset theory is absolutely pertinent to being a head of year. Raising achievement is an unforgiving task – it's difficult and time-consuming, and there will be a time when you feel you have put your heart and soul into a class or a group of students.
- There will be times when you have tried every raising achievement strategy in the book with a group of students and none of it has made a difference… on paper. These are the moments that make or break you as a head of year. The resilient head of year refocusses and refines their efforts to go again. Giving up on students is never an option.

## Personal reflection

Reflect on a time when you have had to be resilient with a group of students when a series of raising achievement strategies have not proved to work. How did you refocus and refine your strategies to bring about improvement?

_____

_____

_____

_____

_____

## Chapter 5 takeaway

### Key points

- Raising achievement is a team game and you must not think that working in isolation is better than utilising the strengths of the various teams of experts in your school. Everyone is working towards the same overall goal; you just need to ensure that, as the linchpin, you pull all the teams together so that all the work that is going on complements each other.
- Understanding key performance data is absolutely vital in this data-driven educational climate. If you don't understand data then you can't understand how your students are performing. Make it your job to be more familiar with student data, what it means and how it demonstrates their performance against similar students nationally.
- School improvement starts with one student at a time in your year group. As the leader of that year group, it is your

job to get your students motivated to perform at the best of their ability. If you succeed at this and your year group all perform, you will have played a very significant part in whole-school improvement.

## Next steps

- **Read**

  Read *100 Ideas for Secondary Teachers: Interventions* by Laura O'Leary. It includes tips for improving academic performance, ways of raising standards of teaching and learning, and plans for promoting a rich culture for learning and high expectations for all learners and specific subgroups.

- **Connect**

  Take time to talk to members of other teams in your school, such as the attendance and behaviour teams or even heads of department. What are their individual goals and how can you collaborate with them so your work complements theirs?

- **Reflect**

  Reflect on your own involvement with the wider teams in your school to date. Are there any teams that you need to work more closely with in order to be more effective in raising the achievement of your cohort of students?

# 6

# Setting standards

---

### CHAPTER OVERVIEW

In this chapter we will look at:

- an ethos of high achievement
- setting and upholding standards
- sharing your expectations and communicating your vision.

---

## An ethos of high achievement

As we have discussed in previous chapters, the role of the modern-day head of year is to ensure that each and every student is not only cared for and looked after but also academically achieving in line with or above expectations. If each head of year takes care of this and gets their cohort to hit the aspirational targets that have been set for them by the school's senior leadership team, the bigger picture of school improvement will take care of itself. School ethos is crucial to make this work and in high-performing schools you can usually 'feel' this ethos when you walk around the building. However, this should not be seen as something that the headteacher or senior leadership team controls exclusively. In simple terms, school improvement and the raising of achievement starts with every single year group being led effectively. As a member of teaching staff, you will be told about and trained to uphold the vision and expectations that the school have, but as head of year it is your job to ensure that this happens.

## *Marginal gains*

A great way to break down big challenges like this is to adopt a 'marginal gains' approach. This approach was made famous by the British cycling team during recent Olympic and Commonwealth Games and focusses on making lots of little improvements that, once aggregated, will result in significant improved performance. This approach is now being adopted by many schools up and down the country. If the head of year can ensure that the day-to-day standards in their year group are consistently being met, then these are the small details that, when added together, will make a big difference to school improvement.

## *Habits*

As we all know, in order to make any improvement sustainable past the initial honeymoon period, whether it's about losing weight or sticking to your new year's resolution, you have to build strong habits. A great quote by Gretchin Rubin, from her book *The Happiness Project* (2011), sums this up perfectly: 'What you do *every day* matters more than what you do *once in a while*.' This is certainly true when it comes to setting standards and building habits that lead to sustainable school improvement. If, as a head of year, you can get the students in your year group to attend, be punctual, bring their equipment, look and feel smart, and give it their all in every lesson of every day, you'll probably not have to worry about the bigger things going on around you. However, if you can't guarantee that, or you don't feel that the little things are important, then you might have a job on your hands trying to get your cohort of students to reach the aspirational targets set for them.

# Setting standards

Every school up and down the country will have their own personal take on what standards they want to see from students and it will undoubtedly look slightly different from school to school. However, in my experience, student standards normally fall into the following areas.

## *Uniform*

Whether your school wants students to wear blazers and ties, or polo shirts and sweatshirts, a high-performing school will want students to stick to whatever uniform policy it puts in place. Students refusing to wear the correct uniform, or who try to make slight adjustments or alterations to the party line, are demonstrating the first sign of not conforming to the rules of the school. In the vast majority of cases, students are consciously doing this to push the boundaries to see what they can get away with. If you turn a blind eye to students bending the uniform rules, don't be surprised when they begin to push other school boundaries even further. Although you might not think that wearing the correct school uniform will make any difference to a child's educational outcomes, if it's the first standard to go because students are beginning to kick back against the school, you are bound to see a drop off in effort and application along the way too. If uniform becomes a barrier for certain families due to financial issues, speak to your senior leadership team about getting a stock of uniform in your office to lend out. Getting a student to feel like they are fitting in by wearing the correct uniform and not being an obvious target for staff every lesson might just be the thing that builds their confidence and self-esteem at school.

## *Attendance and punctuality*

Getting students into school and on time should be your priority when it comes to school improvement. If children are not in the building, then there isn't a single thing on your list of teaching and learning strategies or interventions that is going to help raise their achievement. You need to make it clear to students that even a few minutes late means a few vital minutes of learning time missed. The trick that some schools miss is that they concentrate on attendance due to the legal ramifications but fail to give sufficient prominence to punctuality. What does it say about your school if every single morning you have dozens of students strolling down the road towards your school after the bell has gone, seemingly not bothered about whether they are in on time?

## *Effort*

Although you may not have direct control of what happens in every lesson, you should still be tracking it. If building habits is the route to sustainable success in anything in life, then 100 per cent effort throughout has to be at the core of it. Like Gretchin Rubin said ever so well, it's what we do every day that counts… and for students in school, that means every minute of every lesson, not just the ones they decide to turn it on for. Effort is also something that every student can give, irrespective of their academic ability or starting point. Setting uncompromisingly high standards of effort across your year group is one of the only standards that can never be questioned or challenged by parents. There can simply never be an excuse for a lack of it.

## Behaviour for learning

Often when we talk or think about student behaviour, we tend to think about physical behaviour and disruption. However, these are just the obvious obstructions to learning and resolving them will only go so far when it comes to school improvement. Yes, it's essential to clamp down on classroom disruption and obstructive behaviour, but if you add the words 'for learning' onto the end of the word 'behaviour', you begin to see that there is more to this than just students throwing chairs about and refusing to sit down. Behaviour for learning is the general standard of attitude that our students show towards their studies. I can tell a lot about the behaviour for learning of a class just by looking in their books. What does it say about a student if their book contains graffiti, unfinished tasks, titles not underlined or feedback from a teacher that has not even been actioned?

## Deadlines

The same can also be said for students who miss deadlines for homework submission. What does it say about their attitude to their studies if they refuse to work outside of school, independently of the class teacher? How can you expect those students to prepare themselves for their GCSE exams in Year 11 if they have been able to get away with choosing whether they do homework over the past five years? Getting students into these good study habits from Year 7 usually proves to be invaluable when you require them to work independently as they study for their exams further up the school.

## Equipment

One thing that has bugged teachers for decades is when students come to school without the correct equipment. You've all probably heard the question 'Sir/Miss, can I borrow a pen?' a million times before. If students aren't ready to learn and they are getting away with just turning up to school when they want and without the necessary equipment to enable them to learn, then the whole plan for school improvement is flawed. Standards of equipment and what you expect students to bring are absolutely essential and relatively simple to resolve as long as it's something that you commit to. Some schools try a whole host of ways to resolve this issue, from having stationery shops to issuing teachers with large supplies of equipment to 'lend' students. However, the easiest way that I have seen to reinforce standards of equipment is to simply stipulate in your school uniform policy that students are required to bring a pencil case with them every day to school. If teachers are demanding that pencil cases be out on desks every lesson, then you'll tend to find that those issues begin to go away. However, if you are happy as a school that students are allowed to bring just the odd pen in a blazer pocket, you'll probably always be fighting equipment issues with far too many students.

## Personal reflection

What do these standards currently look like in your year group or at your school?

_____

_____

_____

_____

_____

Which of those standards, if improved, would make the biggest difference to the overall performance of students in your school or year group?

_____

_____

_____

_____

_____

# Sharing your expectations and communicating your vision

Now you've thought about the standards that you need to set and the line that you or your school are going to take on those standards, it's time to share your expectations with students and parents and communicate your vision of how you are going to achieve this with your colleagues. For any school improvement strategy to work, it needs to have 'buy in' from each corner of the golden triangle – staff, students and parents.

If any one of these areas is missing or not effective, you will run into problems sooner rather than later.

## *Staff*

It's one thing having your own set of standards and a vision on how you're going to uphold them across the school, but if you don't share this with the rest of your staff, it's just going to be a one-person crusade. A team is only as strong as its weakest link, so having every member of staff on board is crucial if you want this to work. This can be done in a multitude of different ways and in my experience of doing just this, you need to not assume that just one medium of communicating will be effective. The more people hear the same message and see it in different places, the more it will stick with them. Tell someone something only once and they will either forget it or not attach any real significance to it if it's not reinforced at a later date. We can all say things once, but when you hear someone repeating a key message over time, you begin to see how important it is. Staff briefings, emails and year team meetings are all ways to communicate your vision and ensure that it remains a priority throughout the year.

One mistake that people sometimes make when delivering messages to staff is that the staff don't hear it before the students do. This is usually not intentional, but implies that telling staff has not been that important. For any new strategies or initiatives, take the time to speak to your staff first, so that 1) they feel appreciated and a level of respect and courtesy has been used, and 2) they are ready to uphold any new set of standards as soon as the students have been told. The last thing you want is a 'team' of people who you are hoping will uphold your vision on student standards for you, but who don't feel part of the 'team' because of the poor communication process, so don't make it a priority in their day-to-day interactions with students.

## *Students*

Once the staff know what you are going to say to the students and what you are expecting from them in order to uphold these standards, it is time to inform the students themselves. This needs to be extremely clear and made as simple as possible. If students don't know what is expected from them in terms of day-to-day standards, then they cannot live up to them. The most common way that this is done by a head of year is through assemblies. This is normally the only opportunity that a head of year gets to speak to their whole year group at the same time every week. It's also the most efficient way as everyone is in the same room. However, you need to ask yourself whether it's the most effective way. Just because it's an efficient way doesn't mean to say it's going to be an effective way. Think back to your own school experience when a head of year stood up in assembly and had a rant about uniform or behaviour.

If you want your message to be understood and effective, it's worth thinking about alternative ways to let students know about the standards that you are expecting from them. Methods like using your tutors to speak to students in smaller groups, putting key messages out on your school social media channels and working with targeted individuals are all ways that you can build on your assembly messages. On page 96, I mentioned that staff need to see the same message in a variety of places to start attaching importance to it, and the same goes for students. Tell them once and they'll forget; tell them in different ways at different times and the message will begin to stick.

## *Parents*

Another common mistake we make in school when trying to improve day-to-day standards is to forget to bring parents into the communication loop. Without the support from home, many of the previously mentioned standards will begin to slip, because, after all, children are children and will either start to forget or think about trying to bend the rules. Having a parent at home checking their bag for equipment, making sure they are leaving the house in the correct uniform on time and supporting them to hit their deadlines is absolutely crucial. If parents don't know what you are expecting then they can't help you and are quite right to get annoyed when you pull students up for not hitting these standards. If you communicate your expectations to parents and they are not too far-fetched, the vast majority will support you.

There are a number of ways to communicate your expectations of student standards to parents and, as with staff and students, using several different methods will help reinforce the key messages. Events like parents' evenings and settling-in evenings are great opportunities to get your expectations understood by parents. However, not all parents will attend, so this needs to be followed up by a variety of written and digital communication, such as letters home, parent mailings, social media updates and website articles. It's also important to talk to parents about the 'why'. By letting parents know why you are expecting these high standards and how it all fits with your marginal gains approach or the fact that good habits will, over time, ensure good results, you'll start to win over any parents who may have previously thought you were setting rules for rules' sake.

## Personal reflection

Reflect on an initiative that you led on or that was launched across the whole school. Did you have all corners of the golden triangle working effectively?

_____

_____

_____

_____

_____

Which corner of the golden triangle do you feel you need to improve the effectiveness of in order to make school improvement strategies work more effectively in your year group or school?

_____

_____

_____

_____

_____

# Upholding standards

Trying to uphold student standards well after any launch or battle cry in assembly is always the hardest thing to do. We've probably all seen school strategies that are just a flash in the pan and are here today and gone tomorrow. The job of the head of year in upholding high standards from students is to keep this focus at the forefront of everyone's mind within the golden triangle. There are a number of ways in which you can do this.

## Visibility and presence

Set aside some specific non-contact time to visit the classrooms of your year group and check on standards. This will achieve three main targets:

1  Staff will be reminded about the standards that you expect from your year group.
2  Staff will feel supported in tackling low standards with students from your year group.
3  Students will know that your expectations were not just a load of hot air in an assembly. Both staff and students will know that you are sticking to your word.

Visiting classrooms will also give you the opportunity to see how consistently staff are upholding these standards and where you may need to intervene at a later, more suitable time.

## Tutor time

Although tutor time is traditionally a busy time at the office for a head of year, this is a perfect time to be visible to your year group to support your tutors and reinforce key messages about student standards. If tutor time is first thing in the morning in your school, it's the perfect time to see whether your year group are in school on time and ready to learn with the correct equipment. Scheduling a learning walk once per week in your diary might be time extremely well spent, letting you reinforce standards, support tutors and deal with individual issues before they become even bigger.

## Checking and monitoring

Most schools now have effective systems to monitor attendance, behaviour, attainment and progress. The same should be said for any of the standards you want to uphold. Regular equipment checks are easy to perform and let students and staff know how much importance you are attaching to this. These checks can then be analysed to reveal specific students who are consistently falling below the standards that you are setting, together with specific tutor groups where you feel a form tutor is not prioritising some of these day-to-day standards. The data that you collect will then allow you to put in place individual support and strategies to get both staff and students to meet your expectations of student standards.

## Gate duty

Whilst morning gate duty might just feel like a mandatory safeguarding role, as a head of year you can also use it to reinforce student standards. Telling students that it's great to see them in school on time, or how smart they are looking in their uniform, is all positive reinforcement of the messages that you are trying to get across. Alternatively, speaking to individual students about their timekeeping, or lack of school shoes, school bag or whatever it may be, can be done in a timely fashion before they even enter the school building. If you expect the teachers in the school to uphold your expectations and challenge students who are falling below them, you can't expect them to do this if they know that you are happy to see specific students in your year group walk past you in the morning at the school gate without the correct uniform on.

# Meeting expectations

Joey Kock reflects on how student standards have been a driving force in raising achievement and how, as Achievement Team Leader, she's been able to uphold these high standards day by day, with students consistently meeting her expectations.

## PROFESSIONAL PERSPECTIVE: STUDENT STANDARDS AT THE HEART OF RAISING ACHIEVEMENT

### By Joey Kock, Achievement Team Leader at St Lawrence Academy, Scunthorpe

In my experience as Achievement Team Leader, I've learnt to believe in each and every student because they need to know that you believe in them. They need to know your individualised high expectations and that you'll challenge them regularly about how they are progressing. However, not only do I have high expectations of my students, but I like to start with a personal ethos of high expectations of myself. Students easily pick up on you as their role model. They clearly see that you work hard and tirelessly for them. In response, the majority of students will work just as hard as you do as you are not expecting anything of them that you are not already doing yourself. Here are some of my most basic expectations. I have identified these to be the most valuable and important expectations:

- High expectations of appropriate manners and personal conduct around school.
- School uniform is worn 100 per cent correctly and with pride.
- Attendance is of paramount importance.

- Respect for others, staff and students alike, is required at all times in the school day.

Annually I set one key focus for the year group and make this known to everyone: students, staff and parents. If you want true 'buy in' to the concept, you need to promote it everywhere. It is therefore extremely important to have strong, positive and very open regular contact with parents to share your expectations. I take it upon myself to call parents for any reason – good, bad and indifferent. Getting them to know who I am and what I am expecting of them is vital. I expect the parents to expect their child to be focussed on achieving and participating at all times. I try to communicate my clear expectations for the year groups to parents and make these expectations known to them as soon as possible.

I also don't underestimate the valuable role of a tutor–tutee relationship. In my experience, they are a goldmine of information and your closest link to students. My team of tutors will challenge attendance and behaviour with individual student reports every week. Each half term I will complete a data analysis of the year group with lots of questions seeking answers. Tutors are then provided with this data, and team conversations around year group strengths and weaknesses follow, setting the focus areas for the next term.

Here are some practical ideas for you to think about using:

- Create TLC (tutee learning conversation) cards to allow for target and goal setting and tutor–tutee learning conversations after every report is issued. These conversations are a great way to 'inspire the uninspired' or 'engage the disengaged'. Students will always respond to praise and these students generally will not have had much positive praise. When they see positive statements regularly written down, they begin to see that they are doing something right and this motivates them to continue doing so. Extrinsic motivation begins to become intrinsic motivation.

- Issue student loyalty cards to engage students and specifically target those students least likely to attend revision sessions and students identified as significantly underachieving in key subjects.
- Reward publicly and regularly. Send postcards of praise home for improved attendance, improved achievement or attainment and performing a good deed. Praise progress, but never forget how difficult it is for the very top achievers to show progress. Ensure something uniquely special for them too.
- Establish a solid relationship with subject leaders and know every teacher. Spend time in conversations asking about students and encouraging staff to email you when students have excelled. Make sure to catch up with these specific students with a small reward: a funky pen, pencil, notebook or postcard, or a quick phone call home. Students will quickly begin to realise that you are watching each and every one of them. In this way, they know that you truly care about them.
- Drop into lessons when you are not teaching. Understand where the hotspot lessons are and get to know the more challenging students as much as you can.

## Personal reflection

How confident are you that all of your parents are clear about your day-to-day expectations of your year group?

_____

_____

_____

_____

_____

What more can you do to ensure that your expectations are clear for students, staff and parents?

_____

_____

_____

_____

_____

## Chapter 6 takeaway

### Key points

- Setting and upholding high standards of student attendance, behaviour and performance is a fundamental part of the role of a head of year. If you're going to bother making a rule about it, then you need to make the effort to stick to it. Otherwise it will be the first sign to students that it's okay to be just average and nothing better.

- Communicating your school or year group standards is essential. You might know what you want, but if the rest of the teachers, students and parents aren't clear about it, then you are wasting your time. Take time to use all your school communication methods to outline your expectations so that no one is left in any doubt.

- Upholding these standards can be a constant battle with some students every single day, but it's a battle worth fighting. It's not a battle that you can win on your own though. Use your team of tutors as your foot soldiers.

## Next steps

- **Read**

  Read Chapter 2 of *Leading on Pastoral Care* by Daniel Sobel, which discusses our aims in pastoral care, how your school vision fits into this, together with how we can measure success.

- **Connect**

  Spend time talking to your tutors, students and parents to gain a detailed understanding of how accurate their perceptions are of the standards that you want to achieve. Is everyone singing from the same hymn sheet?

- **Reflect**

  Reflect on the current standards at your school or in your specific year group. How well are they understood by all stakeholders and how well are they upheld? Are there any quick wins that would help improve this?

# 7

# Managing behaviour

---

## CHAPTER OVERVIEW

In this chapter we will look at:

- barriers to learning
- tracking and monitoring student behaviour
- effective sanctions.

---

## Barriers to learning

If you ask any experienced head of year, they'll probably tell you that the vast majority of their time is spent dealing with various types of student behavioural issues. Without doubt this is one of the biggest parts of the job and one that you should be ready for. Experience as a confident classroom practitioner is essential here, allowing you to draw on years of behaviour management experience from your own classes. However, that will only get you so far. Being a head of year is about being a leader and, in this case, that means leading the strategic improvement of behaviour across the whole year group. As with whole-school improvement, if students aren't behaving in classrooms and meeting the student standards that we talked about in the previous chapter, then improved results will almost certainly not follow. In most cases of academy trust takeovers of schools in special measures, the first thing on the agenda of the academy trust is to resolve student behaviour. Without this, the academy will not be able to move forward. Teachers also need to feel supported and will quickly jump ship to another local school if they feel that behaviour issues in classrooms are spiralling out of control and they don't feel they can teach effectively because of the time spent dealing with behaviour incidents. Good schools support their teachers with effective pastoral systems so that they can concentrate on teaching and ensuring their students are learning.

## *Getting to the root of the problem*

One of the biggest failings in our current school system is that, due to the time constraints and pressures of getting results, we sometimes just 'deal with behaviour' and do not spend enough time getting to the root cause of why it is manifesting itself in our classrooms. For lots of behaviour incidents, there's usually a reason behind it. Labelling students as 'naughty students' isn't helpful to anyone and creates a culture where these students are treated purely on the outcome that we see, without looking into what the symptoms leading up to this incident might have been. For classroom teachers this can be extremely difficult – think back to when you were teaching a full timetable. Did you have time to delve into each and every incident of poor behaviour to find out what the root cause was? Probably not, and if your experience was anything like mine, you most likely got significant support from your head of year or the pastoral support team to deal with any issues that arose. Now you're a head of year, this is your job. Has something been going on at home? Is a student playing up in class because they don't understand the work, so negative behaviour is a mask for not knowing what to do? Whatever the reason, if you don't get to the bottom of it then it's probably going to repeat itself further down the line. The time you commit to investigating something to find the real reason behind an outburst or a series of incidents may just be time well spent, so that you don't have to keep dealing with the same problems for weeks on end.

Student behaviour can come in all shapes and sizes and isn't always resolved with the same strategies. Let's take a look at three different levels of student behaviour that a head of year will have to deal with.

## *Low-level disruption*

Although the word 'low' suggests that this may be the least damaging of the three levels, it is probably the hardest one to track and resolve, together with being the one that probably has the most negative impact on learning. When we talk about low-level disruption, we are referring to things like chatting, fidgeting, unnecessary student movement, students easily losing focus and so on. Although each one of these behaviours may not seem like the crime of the century, the problem is that unless they are tackled effectively, they will continue to happen lesson after lesson, ruining any learning atmosphere that has been established in the classroom. These behaviours are almost impossible to track accurately. Again, think back to your own classroom experience. Are you tracking every time a student is talking when they shouldn't be, or when a student is losing focus unnecessarily? As a classroom teacher, you may not know that the same low-level behaviours are being displayed by the same students in every lesson of every day, but as a head of year you need to make it your business to find out. These students are the real reason that your year group won't hit their targets, not the one-off high-level behaviour incidents that are limited to only a few students. If students see their peers causing low-level disruption and effectively getting away with it lesson after lesson, day after day, they will naturally begin to copy this behaviour, causing a culture of disengagement.

## General classroom behaviour

The next level of student behaviour that classroom teachers witness is the general level that teachers find unacceptable and would usually warrant an immediate sanction. This level is often reached once a student has gone past the traditional redirection strategies and warnings from the teacher. These may have been 'the look', the intentional silence or the quiet word. However, if the student has not heeded the teacher's informal warnings, then it begins to move into this level. This is where the classroom behaviour flowchart of sanctions becomes used. Every effective school will have a system for teachers to follow, but as a head of year your job is to ensure that staff are following it consistently and effectively. You can't have some teachers deciding to use it and others not, or even some staff using their own modified version of the flowchart. Consistency here is the key, so the monitoring and tracking of how this is used should become an essential part of your job.

## High-level incidents

In every school, there are times when a very small percentage of students exhibit behaviours that are so serious that the normal classroom behaviour flowchart is not sufficient for dealing with these incidents effectively. These behaviours can either begin as low-level disruption or at the general behaviour level and then progress up to this point due to students refusing to back down at each stage of redirection or sanction; or alternatively they can become high-level incidents immediately with no prior warning or build-up. These are the incidents that you may well be called to respond to immediately or be asked to deal with afterwards. Incidents can range from refusal to obey school rules or challenge to authority to verbal abuse of staff or physical aggression towards staff or students. It is with these incidents that your overview of the whole child is vital. What has led up to this situation? What is going on in their world right now that might have triggered this? What strategies work with this student to get them to calm down? How can you use your relationship with the student as their head of year to resolve this situation more quickly and more effectively than any other member of staff in the school? In some serious situations you may even have to use specific de-escalation strategies and positive handling and physical intervention techniques that you may have picked up from specific training courses such as Team Teach. If you haven't been on any relevant courses yourself, be aware that most schools will have someone trained in Team Teach or an equivalent positive handling course. Speak to this member of staff for some advice on practical de-escalation techniques that don't require any physical intervention. Whatever the outcome, all of these types of incidents will almost certainly come through your head of year office for you to oversee and resolve either immediately or in the medium term.

## Personal reflection

What systems have you currently got in your school to tackle and track low-level disruption? How effective are they at resolving this culture of disengagement?

_____

_____

_____

_____

_____

How consistently is the classroom behaviour flowchart followed by staff in your school? How do you know this? What can you do to improve the level of consistency even further?

_____

_____

_____

_____

_____

# Tracking and monitoring student behaviour

In this day and age, where digital technology is easily accessible in schools, it's simply unacceptable not to have an intelligent tracking system that lets you analyse behaviour incidents in a sophisticated manner. Long gone are the days when teachers used to write behaviour slips out on carbon copy paper, giving one to the student, one to the tutor and one to the head of year. These days, behaviour tracking systems can give you up-to-the-minute 'real-time' information on behaviour incidents across the whole school.

## *Being proactive*

It's one thing having a sophisticated tracking system that provides you with an accurate analysis of student behaviour, but it's another thing using it to be proactive to ensure that the same incidents don't keep repeating themselves again and again. Your job as a head of year is to interpret this information so that you can use it to reduce incidents of poor behaviour and ensure that learning is not affected as a result of it. Knowing about behaviour trends but not doing anything about them is far worse than not knowing about them in the first place. If you've got the information, you need to use it to your advantage to improve the behaviour for learning in your year group. For example, if you know that every Wednesday afternoon in science is not great for your year group, then what are you doing about it? Accepting that next Wednesday is going to be the same, if not worse, is not acceptable.

## *Behaviour trends*

If you are going to be proactive, then understanding the data that your behaviour tracking system gives you is vital. An effective head of year should be able to use the system to spot trends of behaviour happening in their year group. This should include analysis of behaviour trends in the following areas:

- by day of the week
- by time of the day (am or pm)
- by lesson or period
- by subject
- by teacher.

Once you begin to analyse your behaviour trends like this, you will begin to notice interesting patterns that may have not been on your radar before. Is there a specific day of the week that is significantly worse than others? If behaviour is worse immediately after lunchtime, is there anything you can do to combat this? Are there any teachers that require some additional support from your pastoral team?

## *Hotspots*

Once you've got to this level, you can then begin to use the data to predict what is going to happen, taking your strategies to a new level of proactivity. Looking at behaviour on an individual class code level over the past six weeks will probably give you a very accurate indication of where you are likely to see negative behaviour spikes in the coming week. This will allow you to list certain periods throughout the week where you would like a member of the pastoral staff or senior leadership team to drop in, early in the period, to see how things are going. By doing just this and letting the students know that you have called in because there had been some disruption to learning over the past few weeks, you immediately give out the message that this is not going to continue today. Students who may have tried to push the boundaries this lesson will think twice if they know you are possibly coming back to check on them in 20 minutes' time.

## *Subgroups*

Just as achievement and progress are analysed via subgroups, behaviour should be too. Tracking and analysing via subgroup is relatively easy on most modern behaviour tracking systems and gives you some very interesting data to ponder over. Have you got an issue over the behaviour of boys compared to girls? Are your pupil premium students more disruptive than your non-pupil premium students? And are your white, working-class, middle-ability boys the most statistically disruptive subgroup in your whole year group? A few clicks of a button on any sophisticated behaviour tracker should provide you with the answers to all of these questions so that you can spend your time putting your mind to strategies that are going to resolve these issues, instead of manually crunching behaviour data.

## Personal reflection

Which groups of students are the most statistically disruptive students in your year group, or in a selected year group in your school?

_____

_____

_____

_____

_____

How proactive is your school at preventing this subgroup of students from disrupting lessons again in the future?

_____

_____

_____

_____

_____

# Effective sanctions

Schools have a variety of sanctions available to them when dealing with student behaviour. However, as head of year it is your job to review how effective these sanctions are. If a certain group of students are continuing to be disruptive after they have received a specific sanction, it may suggest that this hasn't been effective. The whole idea of sanctions is that they should work as a deterrent for students before they choose to misbehave, or they should ensure that students who receive the sanction don't want to misbehave in the future because they didn't like the sanction they received. Knowing your students is crucial at this point because a sanction that works for one student might not be as effective for another. An experienced and effective head of year will choose from a whole range of sanctions in order to get the best out of their students.

When choosing effective sanctions to give to students, be mindful that they must be in line with your whole-school behaviour policy and must be commensurate with the behaviour issue itself. Nobody wants to see someone excluded for not having the correct equipment with them and equally we don't want to see a student just given a behaviour point if they have verbally abused a member of staff.

The following is a list of sanctions that are usually available to a head of year in any school. Choose between them wisely, based on the incident itself and the behaviour record of the student to date.

## Behaviour points

Normally given by the classroom teacher on the whole-school behaviour system, behaviour points should accumulate throughout the week, month or year. The head of year should analyse these points and intervene when students hit certain thresholds. Behaviour tracking systems should also create league-table-style lists of the worst behaved students in your year group so you can effectively identify and deal with the most persistently disruptive students.

## Detention

Detentions can usually be set by a teacher, head of department or head of year. This may be for a single incident or a build-up of behaviour points over a specific date range. If you set detentions as a head of year, this is certainly one to review in terms of how effective it is. Are the same students on detention every week? If so, what does this tell you about its effectiveness?

## *Phone call home*

For some students the mere thought of their head of year phoning home to speak to their parents or carers is enough to strike fear into them, so much so that they'll never misbehave again. If you know your students well enough, you'll know which ones this works for and which ones couldn't care less. Keeping parents in the loop is crucial though, especially if you're going to count on their support further down the line. Asking for their support and help at home in the early stages might just stop things escalating further.

## *Parental meeting*

When you've used the previous sanctions and a student is still not showing any signs of improvement, you may decide to call their parents or carers in for a formal meeting. This gives you the opportunity to outline how serious this is now becoming and talk about the specific issues that you and the teaching staff are having to deal with. Meetings like this should be documented so that you can refer back to what was discussed if required at a later stage. Sometimes being face to face with you and their parents in a formal meeting is the jolt that some students need. On the other hand, by meeting their parents you might begin to understand why a certain student is behaving like they are.

## *Removal from mainstream lessons*

Most schools have some type of student removal facility from mainstream lessons. This may be a behaviour room or inclusion area. This sanction is typically used for two main reasons. Firstly, this is used so that the student can reflect on their actions and work with pastoral staff to understand the impact that they are having on the rest of the class. The student may also undertake some behaviour modification programmes so that specific behaviour interventions can be put in place to rectify this behaviour. Secondly, this also gives the rest of the class an opportunity to not have their learning disrupted any longer. Seeing a student removed from mainstream lessons for a short period of time can also send a message to anyone else thinking of displaying the same behaviour traits.

## *Fixed-term exclusion*

When a specific student has displayed behaviour that is deemed to be so significant that the internal school sanctions are not appropriate or effective, the headteacher has the power to formally exclude a student for a fixed period of time. Although this may be initially recommended by the head of year or a senior member of the pastoral staff, only the headteacher can officially exclude a student on disciplinary grounds. The headteacher may back your decision and will probably want you to go to them with a possible sanction in mind, but it is only the headteacher who can legally exclude a student. As a new head of year, your headteacher or senior team will probably train you on this, but it is worth always remembering that this line of communication must happen before you make a decision to exclude.

## Alternative education

For a small percentage of students in most year groups, it gets to a stage where they cannot cope in mainstream school and their behaviour begins to reach a point where it is clear that a different education setting and approach is required. Most schools use a range of different providers depending on the specific nature of the student and the barriers to learning that they are facing or displaying. This shouldn't be seen as an out-and-out sanction, but more of a different approach to learning because all of the other strategies have been unsuccessful.

## Permanent exclusion

The final sanction on any school's list of strategies is permanent exclusion. This can only be considered by the headteacher as a last resort, in response to a serious breach or persistent breaches of the school's behaviour policy and where allowing the student to remain in school would seriously harm the education or welfare of others in the school. As a head of year, if this sanction is being considered, you will probably be part of the decision-making process along with the headteacher and senior pastoral staff. Your ability to provide a chronology of events leading up to this point and the behaviour data and analysis on this student will be a key part in making the final decision.

## Personal reflection

Which of the above sanctions have you seen used effectively in your school? What are the reasons for this?

_____

_____

_____

_____

_____

_____

_____

Are there any sanctions that have proved to be ineffective with certain students in your school? What has been done about this? Has another approach been used to bring about improved behaviour?

_____

_____

_____

_____

_____

_____

_____

# Leading behaviour management

Joe Varey reflects on the time when he was a head of year and how he led the strategic management of behaviour across his year group by tracking and monitoring student behaviour in a sophisticated way.

## PROFESSIONAL PERSPECTIVE: THE IMPORTANCE OF ANALYSING STUDENT BEHAVIOUR TRENDS IN PROACTIVE BEHAVIOUR MANAGEMENT

**By Joe Varey, Director of Sixth Form at UTC Warrington**

As a pastoral leader, it is important to recognise barriers that prevent all students achieving their full potential and, for most schools, this tends to involve behaviour. As a good leader, analysis of data is the key to success and implementing plans that lead to positive change. Your interventions in behaviour management are only as good as the data given to you. It is therefore important to identify early trends of behaviour of every student, on a subject-by-subject case, daily and weekly.

At the end of each day as a head of year, I found myself staring at data on the school's management information system (MIS), firstly identifying students who had reached a threshold of behaviour points for that day, then ensuring procedures were followed and that students progressed through the necessary behaviour intervention steps. For me, the most powerful tool is constant and clear communication with parents, so they are clear about our expectations and next steps. This may include a student progressing to form tutor reports, head of year reports or senior leadership reports. When moving students through these intervention steps, it is important that the next person taking responsibility makes that communication with home so that you can maintain a strategic overview.

If a student's behaviour continues to deteriorate, then immediate intervention is vital. Do not allow or accept poor behaviour to continue; you must have a system in place where you can invite parents in to have meetings and ensure you have robust behavioural and pastoral support plans in place. These must be concise as to why the students are at this point in the behaviour intervention steps, with clear, achievable targets for the student that they must adhere to, and consequences if they do not. It is then important to arrange to meet parents within four weeks to discuss their child's progress. Alongside this it is important to keep in touch on a weekly basis to keep the parents informed of any progress or upsets. Keeping this information is vital, as it is usually needed for further steps if that specific student moves on to headteacher or governor behaviour panels.

Once all individual cases have been looked into, the next set of data to analyse is key hotspots throughout the day or week. This entails identifying key areas, timings of the day, subjects, classes and teachers. I would like to point out, however, that it is essential to use this information proactively, not as a tool to point out weaknesses. I have always found this to be an important approach because to change behaviour and culture as a staff team, you all need to work together, so a supportive approach is key. With a supportive approach, you can encourage heads of subject to support at key times or, as most schools now do with an 'on call' system, you can feed this information to the senior leadership team so that there is a key member of staff there to support at the specific hotspots that you have identified.

When analysing behaviour data, it is important to ensure that you are identifying any significant subgroups, such as pupil premium students and students with special educational needs. If you identify significant issues with key cohorts of students, you can call upon expertise from within your school, like the SENCO (special educational needs coordinator), who can look at where support staff may be required within the lessons, to hopefully help minimise poor behaviour within lessons.

Analysis of behaviour on its own will serve one purpose but you should also look to make the link between the impact of a student's behaviour and their progress in lessons. Using this information as a starting point for all conversations and constantly drip-feeding information about the effect their behaviour is having on their progress will have an impact over time. With effective behavioural analysis and appropriate interventions in place, you will see a reduction in negative behaviour and an increase in positive student and staff relationships.

If there is anything that I learnt during my time as a head of year, it is that:

1 Behaviour is not just your responsibility. You need to ensure that there is a whole-school approach and everyone follows and takes responsibility for their part.

2 Quick response is vital. Do not accept poor behaviour and act as soon as you can using the most appropriate intervention.

3 Share your analysis of data on a weekly basis with your wider tutor team. The more they know, the more they can help.

## Chapter 7 takeaway

### Key points

- Getting to the root cause of a specific behaviour issue is absolutely key unless you want to be dealing with the same things day in, day out. Without an understanding of why things are happening, you cannot put any meaningful intervention in place to resolve these issues. All you will end up doing is applying punishments and getting frustrated that they are not having an impact on the behaviour of an individual or a group of students.

- Tracking behaviour trends is just as important as tracking achievement, attendance and anything else your school deems trackable. With the advanced technology now available to us, being able to spot trends and be proactive in your strategies to reduce poor behaviour around school has never been easier. There once was a time when everything was just written down on detention slips. The fact that we now have digital systems that enable us to analyse behaviour trends at the click of a button makes our jobs far easier.

- Picking the right sanction to reflect the nature of the specific behaviour is extremely important. You should also be taking time to analyse the impact of these sanctions. If you are seeing regular repeat offenders receiving the same sanctions every week, it would suggest that either the sanction is proving to be ineffective for those students, or you haven't got to the root cause of the problem, so the sanction you chose is irrelevant.

## Next steps

### ● Read

Read *Getting the Buggers to Behave* by Sue Cowley, which takes a detailed look at the use of incentives for managing behaviour and how to implement a restorative justice approach in order to change children's behaviour. The book also identifies the ten most common forms of misbehaviour and how to deal with them.

### ● Connect

Talk to other heads of year in your school. Are they using any innovative and proactive strategies to reduce behaviour incidents that you could also employ in your year group?

### ● Reflect

Reflect on the different types and levels of sanctions that are available to you as a head of year. Are there any that you could add that may be different to the traditional ones but might have more impact in reducing repeat behavioural incidents?

# 8

# Rewarding effort, achievement and good behaviour

---

## CHAPTER OVERVIEW

In this chapter we will look at:

- intrinsic versus extrinsic motivation
- effective and innovative rewards
- generating a budget to spend on rewards.

---

## Motivating students

Irrespective of whether we are working with children or adults, in education or industry, motivation is a key factor in raising and maintaining performance. If we have got a cohort of unmotivated students, then they are never going to perform in line with the expectations that have been placed on them. A lack of motivation can very quickly turn into widespread disengagement and then the slippery slope to poor classroom behaviour begins. Although each classroom teacher will have their own ways to motivate and engage their students, it is your job as head of year and chief cheerleader to motivate the masses.

If you think back to your own time at school, you may remember that some school leaders ruled purely by fear (and were probably pretty good at it). However, things have since changed in both education and society, and a different approach is now required. Schools and leaders alike have begun to realise that getting the best out of people may require something a little more than just raising your voice from time to time. There should also be an understanding that there is never going to be a 'one-size-fits-all' approach that you can take off the shelf to be effective with each and every student in your school. A great leader will know what works for which student and will deploy their motivation strategies effectively and appropriately to ensure they achieve maximum impact.

## *Intrinsic motivation*

Intrinsic motivation is where a student performs for their own satisfaction through a sense of personal achievement. This is the holy grail of motivation that every school would hope that their students had in bucketloads. Students who are intrinsically motivated want to be better every day because it means something to them and they are driven to achieve for their own personal sense of pride. These students won't ever need a carrot or stick approach because they're not doing it for someone else – they're doing it for themselves. Unfortunately, I've never come across a school that is full of intrinsically motivated students. That's not to say that schools shouldn't be working towards this utopia, for if you ever get there, your job will become a whole lot easier.

Intrinsic motivation also brings with it sustainability, something that real school improvement should be measured against. It's okay to spend thousands of pounds on a shiny new rewards system for a year, but what happens when the budget runs out? What will motivate the students then? Intrinsically motivated students don't require flashy or expensive rewards to perform and can still perform when the going gets tough and there is nobody around dangling a carrot in front of them. However, as we know, this is a place that we'd all like to get to, but is, realistically, some way off for most students.

## *Extrinsic motivation*

Extrinsic motivation is usually driven by the pursuit of an outcome – in this case, a tangible reward. However, the reverse can also apply, where motivation is driven by the fear of an outcome happening – being told off by a parent or teacher, for example. For most of our students, this is what they have been brought up to understand. If you're good, you'll get a merit stamp, some pocket money or a weekend treat. If you're naughty, you'll be told off or lose a privilege. Therefore, breaking that habit and developing them into intrinsically motivated learners is a hard nut to crack. It is this reason why schools up and down the country still base most of their rewards systems on extrinsic rewards.

The significance of these rewards is that they are tangible to everyone. Students can see what they are aiming for and actually get something for their efforts and achievements, and, sometimes more importantly, other students can see that students who have tried harder than them have been rewarded, thus creating a positive domino effect on student motivation. The downside is twofold though. Firstly, rewards can sometimes cost quite a lot of money when you take into account rewards that will motivate the whole school. Secondly, you may find that your rewards system actually creates a negative motivating effect, where students begin to work hard only if they know there's going to be a reward. For example, the teacher says, 'I need you to work harder' and the student replies, 'What's in it for me?'

## *Personal touch*

One thing that has been forgotten by lots of schools since the adoption of high-tech digital rewards schemes is the personal touch. Yes, it may be great for a student to be rewarded with digital points every lesson, giving them the opportunity to save them and then exchange them on the digital platform for a reward that is then delivered to them. But where is the personal touch in all this? For most of us, we probably all remember wanting to please somebody at school. Think back to the time when that teacher had a quiet word with you and told you how well you had done or how proud you had made them. The handwritten note in your book that was personal to you probably made you smile and feel all warm inside. Do any of these digital reward systems do that for our students? Do they get the same feeling when a cheap wristband, key ring or pen is delivered to their classroom from a member of support staff?

In the rest of this chapter, we will discuss a range of rewards that you can use to motivate your students. However, you must always think about how (even if they are based on a digital system where points equal prizes) you can factor in the personal touch. Rewards will mean so much more to children if they involve a human element. It's also important for sustainability (and to avoid a financial crisis) if you can use the personal touch to begin to develop more intrinsic motivation. Although still externally driven, having someone tell you that you've been amazing, or that you've conquered a challenge that they thought was above you, starts to sow the seeds of personal satisfaction.

## Personal reflection

How are you motivated? Are you motivated by extrinsic factors like public rewards or financial incentives? Or are you driven by personal satisfaction more than anything else?

_____

_____

_____

_____

What feels worse when you have made an error of judgement at school – being spoken to by the headteacher or your own personal pride telling you that you could have done better?

_____

_____

_____

_____

# Innovative rewards

When I was at school, the only rewards I can remember were traditional rewards such as merit stamps, certificates in assembly and the odd phone call home. But as I mentioned on page 126, schools are now beginning to think outside of the box when it comes to rewards and are using their imagination and creativity to find rewards that motivate everyone. Not everyone is going to be motivated by a merit stamp in their book and, for some, they'll actually dread the thought of getting up in assembly to collect a certificate. It's vitally important to recognise this as a head of year and not to think that what motivates you (or what once motivated you when you were at school) will motivate the children of today.

Here are my favourite innovative and non-traditional rewards that I have personally used as a head of year or that have been used to good effect in the schools I have worked in.

## Vouchers and gift cards

High street vouchers are a great reward because the recipient can spend them on what they desire, rather than receiving a reward that they might not want. The same goes for iTunes® store vouchers or points cards for games consoles. For a relatively small amount, students can spend these vouchers on one item or put them towards something that they've been saving towards.

## Cinema tickets

Just like with store vouchers, cinema tickets let students pick the film they want to see, meaning that the entire reward is not dictated by the school, leaving a significant element of personalisation to the reward. In my experience, local cinemas are usually pretty good at doing school deals if you are going to buy the tickets in bulk.

## Football tickets

Football can be an expensive game to watch nowadays and can price many families and children out of the market. By speaking to your local football club, you will almost certainly be able to get deals on cheap tickets to take students to home games. In my current school we have bought 11 season tickets to our local football club Middlesbrough. Every home game we take three members of staff and eight students as a reward. Even though we take both boys and girls, if you can use this to motivate your disengaged boys in particular, you may be onto a winner.

## *Local businesses*

You may find that local businesses are an untapped resource. Places such as hairdressers, beauty salons, bowling alleys and leisure centres will be more than happy to provide discount vouchers for their services in return for a picture on your website and social media channels with the student receiving their reward from them. A bit of leg work phoning or calling into local businesses to ask whether they could provide some rewards in return for a mention through your PR channels might just open up a whole new range of rewards that you can offer for a relatively low cost.

## *Prom ticket*

Although specifically related to Year 11, this is usually a great motivator. Lots of schools struggle to find rewards that motivate 16-year-olds because it sometimes feels like trying to buy a present for the person in your life who already has everything. However, with the prom being such an expensive event these days, if a student can work towards having their prom ticket paid for, their family can put that money aside and towards some of the other essentials that tend to be synonymous with that event, such as a suit or dress, matching accessories, limousine hire and so on.

## *Reward rooms*

Games consoles are big motivators in some students' lives, so the chance to play on an Xbox® or PlayStation® with their friends at school might be one that they won't want to miss out on. By committing some of your reward budget on a console, TV screen and a few games, you can create a reward room that selected students can be invited to use before school, at break time and lunchtime and after school. Different year groups can use it every day and invitations can be used as a carrot for certain students who you know will be motivated by this. You may even find that it can help build up relationships with hard-to-reach students. Creating opportunities for teachers and pastoral staff to play against them on the console might just help break the ice with them and help them to see you as real people.

# Free rewards

Not all rewards have to cost money and certainly not all rewards that cost money will be effective. There are a range of different rewards that you can use that are free and that will definitely motivate your students. If all of your rewards have to be paid for, you will need to have significant budget to effectively reward all the students in your year group. The trick here is to be creative and think about what you already have access to on site that you can use to your advantage. With a bit of thought, you will be able to come up with a list of cost-neutral rewards that you can keep giving out every week, without the worry that the pot of money will soon dry up.

Here are my favourite free rewards that I have personally used as a head of year or that have been used in the schools I have worked in to good effect.

## Queue jumper

No matter how old you are, or whether you are intrinsically or extrinsically motivated, everyone loves being able to go straight to the front of the lunch queue. A simple pass system where you give out a certain number of queue jumper tickets per week is a sure-fire winner with students. You might even want to think about adding a 'plus one' to the ticket so that the recipient can take their best friend with them, meaning they don't have to go in for lunch on their own.

## Public praise through social media

The traditional merit stamp in a student's book or a certificate in assembly is rarely seen by many except the student themselves. By utilising the power of social media to publicly praise your students, you begin to widen the reach of this praise and the impact of it. The best use of this is when I have seen teachers take pictures of great work and post it on the school (or subject-specific) social media channels. Not only do other students see this, but family members can also tag wider family (grandparents, family friends and so on) in the post to show how proud they are of that specific achievement. Very quickly a post can be reached by hundreds of people, a far cry from a merit stamp that is just seen by the recipient.

## Cinema club

At various points through the year you might reward students with the opportunity to watch a film in your main hall. Most schools have places where large projection screens and loudspeakers are present, making it the perfect cinema experience for students to watch a movie with their friends. Being invited to this special cinema club is only by invitation though and is perfect when the weather is poor outside, so not only do students get to see a movie with their friends, they also stay warm and dry. You may also find that by taking a significant number of students off the school yard at lunchtime, this also helps with behaviour.

## Hot chocolate with the head

One of the best (relatively) free rewards that I've seen be effective in any of the schools that I've worked in is inviting students to have hot chocolate with the headteacher. This idea was pioneered by Paul Dix and has now caught on nationally, with schools using the hashtag #HotChocFri to post pictures on Twitter every Friday of the student or students who have been nominated for this prestigious reward. If you have not encountered this idea before, take a look on Twitter at the #HotChocFri hashtag and see the amount of schools that are joining in. For students the reward isn't simply to be rewarded by spending time in the headteacher's office, but also to be part of a select group of students nationally every Friday.

## Phone call home

Taking the time to call a select group of parents every week for positive reasons is so powerful. This can be even more powerful if it is a student who you have had behaviour issues with previously, so that parents know that you are just as happy to phone for positive reasons, rather than only contacting them for negative reasons. You may also want to utilise the power of your senior leadership team in this strategy. Asking a deputy headteacher or headteacher to make a couple of phone calls every so often might be the trump card up your sleeve. Even though you are the leader of the year group and the person parents will probably speak to if they have any issues, getting a positive phone call from someone at the very top can be that little bit more special.

## *Praise walks*

As middle and senior leaders, we're usually pretty good at using behaviour points via our tracking systems to know when there are issues in our classrooms. Lots of schools have on-call-style systems where pastoral staff are walking the building and dropping in on classes where negative behaviour points appear. However, how often do you do the same for positive points? Imagine focussing on positive points rather than negative points during one of your learning walks or free periods and dropping in on classes where students are receiving positive points for being super students? The ripple effect of other students seeing students immediately and surprisingly publicly praised like this might begin to change the culture in some classrooms.

# Effective rewards

Whether the rewards you utilise are free or you pay for them, you need to ensure that they are effective. Any school worth their salt will want to know what impact they are having for the money that they are investing. Just like any other intervention in school, you should be able to analyse the impact of your rewards against the financial cost or time commitment that is going into them. In simple terms, rewards that are deemed to be effective and have clear evidence of impact should be used more, and rewards that aren't effective should be used less, or phased out, leaving you that investment to spend elsewhere.

## *Sophisticated analysis*

Just as we discussed in Chapter 7, page 112, about the need to have a sophisticated analysis for behaviour points, the same goes for rewards. If you use the same system for logging behaviour and reward points, then this should be relatively simple. However, are you conducting the same detailed analysis on reward points as you are on behaviour? Looking at the areas that were highlighted in Chapter 7, you should be able to produce a back-to-back analysis of both negative and positive behaviour:

- by day of the week
- by time of the day (am or pm)
- by lesson or period
- by subject
- by teacher.

Your analysis should then identify whether any groups of students are not receiving rewards, whether certain teachers are not giving them as frequently as you'd like and where you need to do some work to ensure a consistent coverage of rewards across your whole year group.

## Personal reflection

What rewards does your school currently use to motivate students? How effective are these rewards? How do you know that these rewards are effective?

_____

_____

_____

_____

_____

Are there any rewards that have been listed in this chapter that you haven't used before and that you feel may work with your students?

_____

_____

_____

_____

_____

# Generating a rewards budget

With school budgets becoming increasingly tighter, often the first things to suffer are pots of money that are seen as non-essential. Staffing and essential classroom resources will always come before rewards, so it is vital to be able to be creative in how you 'top up' any budget that you receive. You may also be reading this and thinking, 'What budget?' If this is the case, then it is even more important to think about how you can generate a rewards budget, or pot of money, that you can ring-fence to reward the students in your year group. Every school has a slightly different approach to this and will prioritise student rewards in a different order depending on the context of the school. However, irrespective of your school's stance on the priority of needing a rewards budget, here are some ways that you can generate extra rewards for your students.

## *Written proposal*

Most schools won't just want to give you a specific amount of money and let you spend it how you wish. The best way to get what you want is to write out a proposal of what you want, how it's going to be spent and, most importantly, what the impact is going to be. If you can demonstrate that you are going to focus some of your rewards on motivating a specific subgroup of students who are causing the school some issues, either academically or pastorally, then you might just get the senior leadership to sit up and listen.

## *Local businesses*

As discussed on page 131, local businesses are often an untapped resource. Most businesses will help where they can because they feel a moral purpose to help children, especially if it is to reward good effort, attendance and behaviour. Being linked in the local press or on your website with projects like this will be great press for them. It may even boost their sales in the long run. Businesses are always offering deals to try to pick up new customers, so why not start with the captive audience you have at your disposal?

## Sponsorship

Similar to the kudos found by local businesses donating rewards and being linked with the school in the local press, sponsorship opportunities for local businesses can bring about the same positive publicity. Even if a local business doesn't feel they have anything to offer your school in terms of a tangible reward, they may be able to sponsor something. I have seen many local companies sponsor awards at school that range from tablets to gift vouchers. Most companies are happy to do so in return for a picture and a comment on your website and social media channels. Inviting a representative from the company to come in and present the award to the specific student is also something to remember. This way the company see the physical benefit of their investment and feel a personal connection to the school, thus increasing the possibility of them sponsoring again in the future.

## Partners

Schools and trusts often have partners that they work with or have connections with. These partners might be in the form of the local council, football clubs or other organisations. All of these partners can probably contribute something to your rewards strategies. A local authority might be able to donate some leisure passes for its local leisure centre, the football club might be able to supply some match tickets and wider organisations may be able to provide other services or experiences. A few emails or phone calls asking for support might be all you need to do.

## Personal reflection

Is your reward budget effective in covering all of the rewards that you want to distribute to your students every year?

_____

_____

_____

_____

_____

_____

_____

How might you look to utilise some of the ideas in this chapter to bolster your budget and increase the rewards at your disposal?

_____

_____

_____

_____

_____

_____

_____

# Strategic leadership of rewards

Making sure that the rewards you use are both effective and age-appropriate is essential in motivating the students in your care. Mike O'Brien reflects on how he has strategically motivated the students in his year group by using a range of effective rewards.

## PROFESSIONAL PERSPECTIVE: MOTIVATING STUDENTS THROUGH THE USE OF EFFECTIVE REWARDS

### By Mike O'Brien, Achievement Leader at Cardiff High School

When I started my role, I inherited a boy-heavy year group of 240 students, with the boys effectively outnumbering the girls two to one. They were beginning that tricky 'in-between' Year 8 period where they had settled after their first year in secondary school but wouldn't make their Key Stage 4 GCSE option choices until the following academic year. As a result, I quickly came to realise that they were generally lacking a bit of motivation and direction and that the normal reward systems in school weren't quite cutting it for them like they did in Year 7.

A specific target for me was to really try to get to know the year group and to understand what made them tick in order to address the issue. Every year group, like every student, will respond differently to every idea. I tapped into the competitive nature of my year group and created a simple house point competition. I used the current school merit system as a base to build upon – every merit earned ten house points and, at the end of the half term, I totalled them all up. Each of the 'houses' battled against each other for a range of relatively inexpensive rewards: the comfy seats during assemblies, free toast once a week during form time and the coveted house point trophy. The end-of-year prize consisted of a free, private and exclusive party with food, drink and a playlist (chosen by them) in our school hall during a lunchtime. The important thing was that the majority of the students actually loved these simple rewards – I listened to student voice to guide me to these decisions.

It worked well as most of the students bought into it and I was able to report the progress and effectiveness of it to the senior leadership team via the improvement in merits earned over the year. As a result, I was able to have a slightly larger budget for the subsequent years as it was proving to yield results. As the students grew older, I tinkered with the system to make it more appropriate for the age of the students. So, by the time they were in Year 10, they were battling it out to go to Oakwood Theme Park for the day. The goal was tangible and (again importantly) something that they wanted – a day in the sunshine with their friends and rollercoasters! For Year 11, I linked their rewards to their end-of-year prom, so that the more house points they earned as a year group meant more exciting additions to the party, such as a photo booth station.

Although this was my overarching vehicle for motivation, it is important to use every opportunity to praise and motivate throughout the year. Therefore, I would make a huge deal of tracking progress regularly and announcing winners in assemblies, tweeting out the victors with pictures and telling the whole staff during briefing who had won and to congratulate them. I would not only focus on the house point competition though, as one approach never works for all. I would always try to celebrate different students' achievements in every assembly, no matter how big or small they may be. Even though I was the 'Head Cheerleader' for the year group, it worked best when my 'Cheer Team' (or form tutors) were on board and celebrating their successes too. We even turned it into a bit of a competition amongst the tutors so that they all bought into the idea and became motivators in their own rights as well.

However, despite this larger house point idea, one of the most powerful and simplest tools in your arsenal is to be personable and personal with your students. A simple comment about something they've done well, a handshake

or merely showing an interest in their lives ca
student hugely – sometimes much more than the
a tangible prize. For a student to know that you're t
interest in them, when potentially other adults in the
don't, can make the world of difference.

Overall, I would advise:

- Getting to know your year group as a whole and as individuals – find out what makes them tick.
- Use every opportunity to celebrate their successes, in school via assemblies and so forth, but also with phone calls home and on social media.
- Try to give school that 'fun' edge of having something else to aim for rather than it being solely grades or levels – reward everything that you can.
- Galvanise your tutor team so that you can delegate the role of motivator to them also.
- Every student is an individual and will respond differently to different types of motivation – be personal.

## Chapter 8 takeaway

### Key points

- There is no one-size-fits-all approach for how to motivate students. Some will be intrinsically motivated, and some will require extrinsic motivators. The key is to know your students inside out and select the right rewards and motivators to ensure you get the very best out of the students in your care.
- Effective rewards don't always have to have a monetary value. There are many ways to reward students and show them that you are proud of them for their efforts and achievements. Think creatively about all the different

ways you can reward your students with the tools at your disposal.

- Topping up any school budget you have for rewards can be done in a number of different ways. Explore the partnerships that your school may have and speak to local businesses. You may just find organisations that are falling over themselves to be connected with a good news story about students' achievement.

## Next steps

- **Read**

    Read *When the Adults Change, Everything Changes* by Paul Dix for a comprehensive look at how to build positive relationships with students, shaping their behaviour through your own.

- **Connect**

    Take time to speak to students and ask them what motivates them. Listening to student voice is vital when trying to design rewards that motivate your students. If you only design rewards that you think will motivate your students, you might be way off the mark.

- **Reflect**

    Reflect on some of the rewards that your school have previously used for different year groups. Which rewards motivate the students the most? And which have failed to motivate?

# 9

# Attendance and punctuality

---

## CHAPTER OVERVIEW

In this chapter we will look at:

- using attendance to raise achievement
- understanding why students don't attend
- utilising your attendance team.

---

## The first step in raising achievement

The first step in any raising achievement plan should be to get students in the building. Put simply, if students aren't in the building, then they are missing out on valuable learning time. You can put all the intervention sessions on you want and create highly complex learning strategies in the classroom, but if students aren't there to benefit from it, then you are wasting your time. However, this is sometimes overlooked by schools because it almost seems too basic for someone who is trying to think outside the box to bring about change. As a head of year, it is your job to do everything that you can to get your students in the building, so that all of the other school improvement strategies can impact upon them.

## Research

The link between attendance and achievement isn't just an idea that might work for some schools; it is backed up by significant Department for Education research and published reports. In 2012 the Department for Education published the report 'Improving attendance at school' (Taylor, 2012), highlighting that 'there is a clear link between poor attendance at school and lower academic achievement'. It goes on to explain that only three per cent of pupils with attendance of under 50 per cent manage to achieve five or more GCSEs at grades A* to C including maths and English, and 73 per cent of pupils with over 95 per cent attendance achieve five or more GCSEs at grades A* to C. The Department for Education then added to this in 2016 when they published the report 'The link between absence and attainment at KS2 and KS4' (Department for Education, 2016). In this report, the Department for Education delved deeper into the statistics, especially for students with only ten to 15 per cent absence. The report demonstrated that 'pupils with no absence are 1.3 times more likely to achieve level 4 or above, and 3.1 times more likely to achieve level 5 or above, than pupils that missed 10–15 per cent of all sessions' (p. 12).

## Pupil premium students

This is even more significant for your pupil premium students, as nationally pupil premium students' attendance is, on average, approximately three per cent less than their non-pupil premium counterparts (in 2016–17, national non-pupil premium absence was 5.4 per cent, whilst pupil premium absence was 8.8 per cent; Department for Education, 2018a). Although we will talk about closing the gap in Chapter 11, page 177, your first closing the gap strategy based on national statistics for attendance should be to improve their attendance. That is certainly a strategy that my current school have employed and to very good effect. Prioritising pupil premium students to call first on a morning when you're making your 'first day response calls' for absences costs nothing extra but might start to chip away at the attendance gap in your school.

## *Educating parents*

One of the biggest challenges when it comes to attendance is educating parents. As I mentioned in Chapter 5, page 79, for years at school, or in any other walk of life, a score of nine out of ten, or 90 per cent sounds great. We've all been told that 90 per cent plus is outstanding. You therefore can't really blame parents for thinking that an attendance record for their child of 90 per cent is not a problem. However, as we all know in education, this certainly isn't good enough when it comes to attendance. But do you do enough to educate parents on this? Have you taken enough time and effort to educate parents on the fact that a 90 per cent attendance record means that their child is missing one day of school per fortnight? When you begin to explain it in terms like this, it starts to hit home. Getting your school to put out regular motivational messages like this on the school website and social media channels will hopefully add a little bit of education behind why you want their children in school every day.

## *Punctuality*

Punctuality is something that should not be overlooked when thinking about attendance. It relates directly to Chapter 6, page 92, on setting standards, where I asked the question: 'What does it say about your school if every single morning you have dozens of students strolling down the road towards your school after the bell has gone, seeming not to be bothered about whether they are in on time?' As schools, we are preparing young adults for life in the real world, so we have a duty of care to them to make them understand the importance of being on time for school or work, not to mention how disrespectful it is to colleagues if you are late in a working environment built on collaboration and team trust. We should therefore be monitoring and analysing punctuality data in the same way that we are tracking attendance figures. Groups of students, individuals and interesting trends should be looked at in an attempt to understand the data and then do something to improve it.

### Personal reflection

How much of a priority is improving attendance in your whole-school or year-group improvement plan?

_____

_____

_____

_____

_____

_____

How do you educate parents on the importance of attendance at school?

_____

_____

_____

_____

_____

# Understanding why students don't attend

Improving attendance has to be done with one student at a time, but, before you can begin to improve the attendance levels of any one student, you need to know the reasons behind why they aren't attending in the first place. Until you get to the root cause of the problem and identify the barriers to getting them in the building more regularly, then most of your efforts will probably be unsuccessful. Taking time to find this out will be time well spent in your overall aim to improve achievement, rather than just taking a scattergun approach to school improvement. Find out what is stopping them from attending and then put your efforts into trying to remove these barriers, so they attend more regularly.

Although there are many individual reasons why students don't attend school more regularly, here are some of the more common reasons that I have found from being a head of year and things you might be able to do about it.

## Friendship issues

Friendship issues are the bane of every head of year and usually take up the most time to resolve. From minor 'fallings out' to large-scale disagreements that turn nasty, the result can sometimes be non-attendance at school for a few days. Any parent will want to protect their baby, so when a student tells their mum or dad that they don't want to go to school because they have no friends, or that there was a big public falling out yesterday, sometimes parents will keep their child off until it either blows over or the school does something about it.

These issues can be extremely difficult to diagnose and deal with, as in most of the cases that I've been involved in, there isn't usually one party that is completely blame-free. When friends fall out, usually things have been said by both sides and other children within the friendship group decide to side with one person or the other. Getting everyone together to forget what has happened, clear the air and agree to move on is your job as peacemaker. The quicker you can get that student back into school, the better for everyone.

## Bullying

Although it's currently rarer than it ever has been in schools, bullying still exists but sometimes in a slightly different form. Gone are the *Grange Hill* days where students would have their dinner money taken off them every day and their heads flushed down the toilet. Students now operate in more covert ways to bully others. Sly comments when nobody is around, spreading false rumours and constantly targeting certain individuals for ridicule is how bullying can pan out in today's society.

Suddenly noticing a drop in someone's attendance, coupled with piecing together the fact that they haven't been their jovial self recently, can be an alarm for a case like this. Sitting down with the student and their parents and trying to get to the bottom of why they aren't attending is vital. Conversations like this can open up a whole can of worms, but at least when it's all out in the open you can do something about it.

## *Social media*

Very much linked to the last two reasons, social media can play a huge part in both friendship issues and incidents of bullying. Calling someone a name on the playground is one thing, but having an embarrassing photograph or a nasty rumour plastered all over social media is another thing entirely. Not wanting to show your face in school for days afterwards is quite common for teenagers. The embarrassment of turning up to school to be ridiculed in public, after the night of digital ridicule that they have just had to suffer, is not something that many young people want to endure. Instead, most try to lie low for a few days and hope that it will all go away.

This can be one of the trickiest situations to resolve, because once a rumour or photograph has left someone's computer or mobile device, there is no way of finding out where it has gone. The social media domino effect is so quick that you have no control over who has liked, shared or taken a screenshot of it. All you can try to do is to get to the source as quickly as you can, get them to remove it and then educate them on why this is not appropriate (so as not to be in the same position again in a few weeks' time).

## *Disengaged students*

From time to time, and generally as students move up through the school, some students become disengaged with school and begin to vote with their feet. This may be because of a lack of parental support to get them into school, a lack of exciting lessons from their teachers, or something completely different. National statistics reflect this trend in higher absence rates as students get older, with absence rates between Years 1 and 7 being approximately four per cent, increasing to five per cent between Years 8 and 9, and then rising to six per cent for Years 10 and 11 (Department for Education, 2018a).

Knowing each and every one of your students is key to understanding what makes them tick or, in this case, what is not making them tick. What is it about their diet of education at your school that is not motivating them to get out of bed in the morning and put on their uniform? Is it a friendship issue like we discussed in the previous two points, or have they been 'turned off' by the GCSE option choices that they have made? Either way, sitting down with them and looking at what you can do to re-engage them is essential for any high-performing school. You may not be able to remove some of the barriers (for example, 'I hate maths'), but there are always things you can do to work with the student and effectively meet them halfway in a deal to get them back into school.

## *Illness*

Although illness can't usually be helped, there are lots of 'illnesses' that don't require students to be off school. Students taking days off for minor headaches, sore throats and general aches and pains are usually backed up by their parents, who are happy to keep them off school for trivial illnesses like this. In this instance, half the battle is educating the parents on what is acceptable to stay off for, and what students can probably cope with in lessons. For example, would a sore throat stop you from learning? In some cases, parents may thank you for backing them up with their child when you say that you want them in school. This way, it means that they don't have to take a day off from work to look after them.

Some of these 'illnesses' may also be a mask for a separate issue, such as a friendship problem, bullying, disengagement and so on. Parents themselves may not have realised the bigger picture behind these absences, but when you start to look at a pattern of absences where a student is having a day off every couple of weeks for a range of low-level illnesses, you may begin to wonder whether there is something hiding behind the illness.

## Personal reflection

Think about a specific student who has been off quite regularly or who has demonstrated a pattern of absence over a longer period of time. How well do you think you understand the reasons behind these periods of absence?

_____

_____

_____

_____

What more can you do to remove these barriers, so that this student can begin attending more regularly?

_____

_____

_____

_____

_____

# Utilising your attendance team

Although all schools are different sizes and therefore they will have different staffing structures, you will usually find that due to the statutory nature of school attendance, each school will have some type of attendance team made up of support staff. These teams may include such roles as an education welfare officer (EWO) and attendance managers, plus the possibility of a senior leader having overall responsibility for whole-school attendance. So, although you may feel that attendance for your year group is your responsibility, you should not feel that it is a one-person crusade. If your school is anything like any of the three schools that I've worked in, then you'll have extremely skilled and willing support staff, ready to try everything in their armoury to get students into school and learning. Given strategic direction from a forward-thinking and creative head of year, your attendance team can turn into sleuth detectives, identifying patterns and trends of absence and improving attendance along the way.

Whether you're working alone or with your EWO or members of your wider attendance team, here are some key areas for you to focus on when looking to improve attendance, based on my own experiences.

## *Working with families*

There are only a few families I've come across who just don't want to send their children to school for no reason at all. Most families, deep down, want their children to come to school and receive an education, but other factors may get in the way. Whether it is due to poverty and not being able to buy the correct school uniform, not being able to get to school on time due to caring for a family member, or parents feeling that they need company or support at home, there is normally something that a school can do to help. Working with families in this way will help not only attendance but achievement too. Trying to resolve wider family issues, or at least pointing them in the direction of specialist help, can unlock the door to everything else. Although you may not have the experience or knowledge of where to access this type of help to resolve some of these issues, all schools have access to extended teams of professionals who are trained to deal with these types of scenarios. A quick phone call to the relevant people can sometimes be all that is required.

## *Identifying previous issues*

There's a fair degree of reliability that if students (or families, more to the point) have had significant previous attendance issues at either your school or their primary school, they will probably continue to do so. This is directly related to the previous point about working with families. If the root cause (a family issue) has not been diagnosed or resolved, then the issue will most likely continue to happen, resulting in continued poor attendance. Looking into previous data and already identifying and targeting certain families is where attendance and punctuality work can be proactive rather than reactive. Putting support in place before things go wrong with vulnerable families is intelligent work. Sitting back, waiting for it to happen and then saying, 'They had attendance issues at their previous school too' is poor middle leadership. Effective schools are already working with identified families of Year 6 students before they even arrive in Year 7.

## *Sophisticated data analysis*

Just as I've already discussed in Chapters 7 and 8, either you or your data team need to be able to conduct an accurate and sophisticated analysis of attendance and punctuality data. Most schools now have extremely skilled and competent data teams who are able to churn out data on anything that moves. Just like behaviour and rewards, your attendance and punctuality analysis should be able to be broken down into multiple subgroups and matched against both school and national targets. Only then will you be able to truly ascertain how good your year group attendance picture is and how effective your improvement strategies have been. Over recent years, targets have been introduced for areas such as persistently absent (PA) students – students with an absence rate of ten per cent or more across an academic year. There is also now a greater focus on closing the gap between pupil premium and non-pupil premium students, along with a greater scrutiny on gaps between boys and girls; all of this will be discussed in Chapter 11, page 177. A sophisticated analysis system should be able to identify these groups at a click of a button, enabling the head of year to make sense of the data and then work with their wider attendance team to remove any barriers that exist.

## Personal reflection

How good are you or your school at working with families to resolve some of their wider issues that may be impacting on their child's attendance at school?

_____

_____

_____

_____

_____

How proactive are you or your school at identifying previous attendance issues and ensuring that they don't continue when students arrive at your school?

_____

_____

_____

_____

_____

# Sustainable improvements

Getting to the root cause of attendance and identifying any barriers to attending school are both vital if you are going to make sustainable improvements in attendance. Adele Mulligan reflects on how she has effectively worked with families to bring about improved attendance.

## PROFESSIONAL PERSPECTIVE: WORKING WITH FAMILIES TO IMPROVE ATTENDANCE

### By Adele Mulligan, Head of Year at St Michael's Church of England High School, Liverpool

As a head of year in a school with a high proportion of pupil premium students, attendance is a principal focus for us all. From the outset, attendance is emphasised as important with all parents and carers. At our induction evening, attendance is one of our key foci during the presentations made by senior leaders, with actual examples of students whose grades were affected by their poor attendance as well as a clear demonstration as to what 90 per cent attendance will mean over the course of the five years students spend with us.

For those students who have been identified as having low attendance in primary school, it is important that you connect with those families as soon as possible, whether it is a phone call before the end of the term (before they start) or a meeting in school. This way you can pre-empt any issues before the student starts, and it sets up a good foundation for a positive relationship in the future. As a head of year, I believe positive relationships are vital, especially when having to have difficult conversations regarding behaviour or attendance. If parents or carers trust you, students are more likely to trust you. Therefore, they will approach you with any difficulties in school rather than feigning illness or staying off.

First-day response is imperative to keeping on top of attendance. My school uses a system that sends out a text or email if we haven't had a reason for a student being off, and parents respond well to it. This reduces the number of unauthorised absences. As a head of year, if I have a concern about a student who is off, I ask the attendance officer to ring them directly. In addition, if a student does have two or more days of unauthorised absences, our attendance officer will do a home visit. It is crucial that you know why a student is absent. Our attendance officer produces a report at the end of every day with information on both authorised absences and unauthorised absences. I ask for medical evidence if a student is absent on numerous occasions for the same reason. If there are issues in school, they become a priority.

A student cannot make progress if they are not in school, so therefore getting them into school is pivotal. If the issue is with their peers, parents are encouraged to bring students in to meet with myself or a learning mentor, and students are offered a safe place to work until they feel the issue has been resolved. The important thing is that they are in the building. Through experience, the longer a student is absent due to worrying about these issues, the harder it is for students to come back. Dealing with these issues as soon as they arise means that they don't have a chance to build up their anxiety.

If there is no improvement in attendance without any real valid reason, our next step is an attendance panel. Parents are invited in to meet with staff on a graduated scale, starting with the attendance officer and working up to the headteacher if no improvement has been made. Here staff will highlight issues with attendance and any patterns, and they will develop an action plan along with parents, which is then signed by parents in the meeting and can therefore be referred to by staff if they have more conversations regarding that particular student's attendance in the future.

In terms of encouraging students, I have found the best way to be a bit of competition. I run an inter-form competition that offers a form class a reward on a termly basis. This can be a film afternoon with popcorn and juice, a party at Christmas or even a discount on a trip. Attendance is drilled into students in every assembly and the competition is displayed. This results in students becoming very competitive and encouraging each other to attend school.

In short:

1 Know your students from the outset – if they have poor attendance in a previous school, it's likely to continue.
2 Meet or introduce yourself to the parents – a good relationship with them is key.
3 Know why students are not in school.
4 Do everything you can to get students into school, whether this is in class or somewhere they feel safe.
5 Deal with issues that affect attendance as a matter of priority.
6 Deal with poor attendance – don't just ignore it. Flag any patterns with parents or carers and get an agreement in writing that you can refer to further along the process.
7 Engage the students – use competitions and rewards as an incentive.

## Chapter 9 takeaway

### Key points

- Getting students in the building is the first step to raising achievement. If they're not in the building, they're not learning. Before you think about any other school improvement strategies, make sure that you get as many students as possible across the doormat every single day.
- There's always a reason behind why a student does not attend school; you just have to search for it. Work with their family and take time to understand their reasons for not wanting to come to school. Then do everything in your power to remove these barriers for either the family or the individual student.
- Don't underestimate the capability of the support staff in your school. Use their time, energy and significant expertise in data processing and analysis to produce a sophisticated analysis of attendance that lets you understand where your issues are compared to school and national targets.

### Next steps

- **Read**

  Read *Improving School Attendance* edited by Eric Blyth and Judith Milner. This book includes research material on improving attendance at both school and local authority level.

- **Connect**

  Speak to the support staff who make up the attendance team in your school. Take time to discuss your vision for attendance in your year group with them so they can be as effective as they can for you.

- **Reflect**

Reflect on previous instances of poor attendance that you've either been involved with or have seen. What were the root causes for this? Is this something that could have been predicted from prior data? And did you or the school do enough to resolve this to create sustained improvements in their attendance?

# 10

# Safeguarding and student welfare

---

## CHAPTER OVERVIEW

In this chapter we will look at:

- keeping children safe
- the wider remit of safeguarding and student welfare
- responding, recording, reporting.

---

## Keeping children safe

The most important part of any teacher's initial training or ongoing professional development is safeguarding. There are so many strategies and techniques that we are told to do, use and develop in our classrooms, but there are not many that are statutory. In 2019, the Department for Education in England published statutory guidance detailing how all schools and colleges in England must act when carrying out their duties to safeguard and promote the welfare of children under the age of 18 (Department for Education, 2019a). I'm sure that you will have seen this document and be familiar with it, just like the rest of your staff. However, as a head of year, due to the nature of some of the issues that you will oversee in your year group, it is vital to know this document inside out and not just at surface level.

One of the things I remember from being a younger, less experienced teacher coming into the profession is that I was always comforted in the knowledge that there was a team of more experienced professionals in the school to help me with things I wasn't sure about. As a form tutor, this meant having a head of year I was confident to go to for advice or to resolve an issue that I didn't have the skillset to resolve myself. If we take safeguarding as an example, I would have read the statutory guidance as an overview of what my responsibilities were as a teacher, but I would have known deep down that if a situation came to light in relation to safeguarding, or if I wasn't sure where the threshold was, I would have always gone to my head of year for guidance, advice and support. Now that you are that person, you need to have a far deeper understanding of safeguarding and student welfare so that you can support your team in doing what is right for the children in your school.

## *Linchpin*

Right back in Chapter 1, page 74, we discussed how the role of the head of year is absolutely vital in the academic and pastoral development of each and every child in your year group. Your role as a linchpin for their wellbeing is never more important than in times where safeguarding and student welfare is of concern. As stated in the aforementioned 2019a Department for Education guidance, 'No single practitioner can have a full picture of a child's needs and circumstances and, if children and families are to receive the right help at the right time, everyone who comes into contact with them has a role to play in identifying concerns, sharing information and taking prompt action.' What this highlights is that a single teacher, tutor or leader can never have enough information to make a decision on their own about a significant concern over a student's welfare. However, what this also indicates is how important the head of year is in these situations, because they are the person with the best overview of the child, the concerns and any other contextual information.

## The jigsaw and the puzzle

A good head of year will fit together all of the information that they know on a student and be in a far better position than any other member of staff to make a recommendation (in connection with the designated safeguarding lead) on what to do next. Sometimes even the smallest of details, or the issues that many teachers may feel are too trivial to report, could just be the missing piece in the jigsaw for the head of year. It is this information that may be the final piece in the jigsaw that enables the head of year to access the help and support that a child needs. Due to this, the role comes with great responsibility for the welfare of each and every one of your students. If you ask any parent what the number one thing is that they want from the school for their child, they will probably all tell you that care, safety and happiness are at the top of their list. So, as head of year, it is vital that you are clear about this and that you are constantly looking out for the welfare of your students and keeping your eyes and ears open for anything that may be telling you otherwise.

## The wider remit of safeguarding

When I first started teaching nearly 20 years ago, safeguarding and student welfare were all just about the three main types of abuse that students may come into contact with – physical, emotional and neglect. However, in recent times, this has developed much further with the inclusion of radicalisation and the Prevent agenda. In 2015, the Department for Education

issued schools and colleges in England with advice relating to
the 2015 Counter-Terrorism and Security Act. This guidance is
intended to help schools think about what they can do to protect
children from the risk of radicalisation and prevent people from
being drawn into terrorism. What this now means for a head
of year is that it is essential that you and your team are able
to identify children who may be vulnerable to radicalisation
and know what to do if this is the case. Being able to protect
children from the risk of radicalisation is now part of your wider
safeguarding duties.

## Personal reflection

To what extent are you knowledgeable on your responsibilities
for both keeping children safe and preventing radicalisation?

_____

_____

_____

_____

_____

Are there any areas that you don't feel comfortable with?
If so, where can you get the extra support, advice or
information that you need in order to feel fully competent in
these key areas of safeguarding?

_____

_____

_____

_____

_____

# Responding, recording, reporting

Within your school there will be a designated safeguarding lead who will ultimately be responsible for judging whether a particular issue has crossed the threshold into becoming a safeguarding situation. They will also be the ones who will probably make any referrals based on the information you give them. However, you will undoubtedly play a big part in getting to that stage. In my experience as a head of year, your involvement will be most likely to have come because of one of two reasons:

1  A tutor or teacher comes to you with some concerns that they have about a student in your year group. These concerns may have come because of a disclosure from a student, some information they have been told or heard, or something they may have picked up from reading their work.

2  A student in your year group speaks to you directly about an issue that you deem to be of a safeguarding nature. This may stem from you investigating a specific incident in or out of school, or a student coming to you independently because they want to disclose something.

Irrespective of how the issue arises, you have a duty of care to respond in a way that meets the statutory guidance issued by the Department for Education and your own school policy. This is where you'll begin to match all of the pieces of the jigsaw puzzle together and make a judgement on whether to involve the safeguarding lead, depending on the nature and significance of the information you have. However, the way you respond, record and report is absolutely key in this process.

## *Responding*

Although you will have been trained on what to do and how to respond (or how not to respond) as an individual member of staff if a child discloses something to you, you may not have had the same level of training on what to do if it comes second hand to you via a colleague. As I mentioned earlier in this chapter, approaching a more senior figure in the school because you may not know exactly what to do yourself means that if somebody comes to discuss a concern with you, then they need your help and advice. One of the things that I've learned from countless situations like this is to take my time and not to be swayed by someone's emotions. Just because a member of staff is upset or angry doesn't mean to say that what has made them feel this way is a cause for immediate action. Sometimes the closer you get to a situation, the harder it is to make an objective judgement on it. By taking your time, listening carefully and then piecing together all the information, together with the other contextual information that you hold on that student, you can come to an objective decision based on the facts and your intelligence as head of year. If you rush in too quickly and are swayed by people's emotions, you can often make knee-jerk reactions that you'd never make if you had just had the opportunity to take a step back in the cold light of day.

There are, however, times when you do need to act straight away when you feel that a child is in immediate danger. No matter what is happening in school, whether you are teaching or whether another member of staff who has just passed on their significant concerns is teaching, if it involves a child in immediate danger, everything stops and this must be your sole priority. This clearly needs to involve good judgement from the outset because, as we have just discussed, making a knee-jerk reaction every time someone came to share a concern would mean that you'd be constantly on red alert. Luckily, the more experience you get as a head of year, the easier it is to make these decisions about when someone is in immediate danger and what constitutes a safeguarding concern.

You must also remember though that your job isn't to be detective and see the concern through from start to finish. Within your school you will have a designated safeguarding lead and probably a team of support staff who are highly skilled and well trained to deal with situations such as this. Once you've responded accordingly and obtained the necessary information you require, it is then time to pass this on to the designated safeguarding lead, who will take over from there. In certain circumstances they may want or need you to continue helping with the situation, especially if it is quite a significant issue (therefore you will need to drop everything you were about to do), but on other occasions it may be fine for you to go back to doing what you were doing before this information came to light. If you are needed to stay with the student, SENCO or designated safeguarding lead, then a quick call to your office manager or cover manager to get any lessons covered will be what is required.

## *Recording*

Just as you would if you were recording information given to you by a student during a disclosure, it is good practice to do exactly the same if a teacher comes to you with a concern that you feel may reach the safeguarding threshold. Writing down exactly what they say and in their words is always good, so that you know that you haven't influenced the situation at all. In schools these days, this can be made so much easier due to the aid of digital communication and recording platforms, together with email. Asking someone to write down their concern on either of these two mediums means that not only do you have their concern written in their own words, but there is also a paper trail to go with it, along with a time and date. This is particularly important if an incident goes forward under a significant child protection case.

One thing to remember though, if you receive information such as this in a written form, is to also speak face to face with the person submitting their concern. Words can be easily misconstrued, taken out of context, played down or exaggerated when reading them cold. I have seen instances where an email has been written like the world is about to end when it isn't, and vice versa. The important thing to do is to read the information, digest it and then look to speak to that member of staff as soon as possible to fill in any blanks and get a sense of how serious this situation is. You can't question an email or a written statement, but you can when you are speaking to someone face to face.

Once you are happy that you have all the information you require, then you need to make that judgement of whether it has crossed the threshold. However, don't feel that this is something you have to do on your own. Although you may feel you want to make the right decision and not bother the designated safeguarding lead when it does not constitute that, I'm sure they would be more than happy for you to discuss the issue with them if you are unsure, rather than them having to pick up the pieces later down the line because you take the decision not to progress it on your own and it turns out to be a bad decision. After all, if you are a new head of year, you will no doubt need to talk it over with someone who has more experience than you in this area. Talking it over and finding out that it doesn't constitute a safeguarding concern will also be a good training exercise for you moving forward in your role.

# *Reporting*

As we've just discussed, once you have information that has been passed to you from a colleague, or you have received a disclosure directly from a student, then you have a responsibility to pass this on to your designated safeguarding lead. Keeping this information to yourself is dangerous, may well cause you to lose your job and, depending on the significance of the information you receive, is potentially against the law. It is vital to make sure that you have followed the previous two steps in ensuring you have responded correctly, recorded the information accurately and then reported this to your designated safeguarding lead. Once this has happened, you will then be directed by the designated safeguarding lead as to what involvement you will need to have.

When all this is happening and the pressure is on to help a child in need, you can often forget to do one of the most important parts of the process. That is going back to the person who initially passed on their concern to you, to thank them for the information and to let them know that you took their concern seriously and passed it on to the relevant people. By doing this, not only are you showing respect and courtesy to your colleagues, but you are also giving them confidence that the system works. The last thing you want when working with a team of teachers or tutors is that they have a perception (rightly or wrongly) that their concerns never get acted on. All this does is put doubt in people's minds about whether to bother passing on any more concerns if they think that they are never looked at. There will be many details that will be confidential about the situation that you won't be able to feed back to them, but just having them know that you appreciate that they took the time to raise a concern about one of your students will go a long way to making them feel that it was worth it, even if it didn't go any further.

### Personal reflection

Have you ever been in a situation where you have reported a concern up the line of command in a school and not received any feedback afterwards? How did this make you feel?

_____

_____

_____

_____

_____

_____

What factors sometimes make this tricky? How can you build systems to ensure that you communicate with the people raising significant concerns once a decision on what to do has been made?

_____

_____

_____

_____

_____

_____

## Growing in confidence

Safeguarding can be one element of the job that some people find scary. Jamie Wordsworth reflects on how, even as an inexperienced head of year new to the post, he was able to work closely with his more experienced colleagues and quickly grow in confidence in his new role.

## PROFESSIONAL PERSPECTIVE: SAFEGUARDING IS NOT AS SCARY AS IT SEEMS

### By Jamie Wordsworth, formerly Head of Year and currently Deputy Headteacher at The Castle School, Taunton

As an inexperienced teacher only in my second year of teaching when I took on the role of head of year, I had very little knowledge or understanding of anything more than the basics of safeguarding. As a classroom teacher, I knew the signs of abuse and I knew how to report them to the designated safeguarding officer if I had concerns about a student. My school was very good at safeguarding training and I was very informed of the procedures that were in place to safeguard young people. Probably quite naively, I didn't really consider that being a head of year would result in becoming more involved with the safeguarding of students. Once I did come to realise that, it was the part of the role that caused me the most worry. Safeguarding initially felt like something that I could get wrong and, if I did, the consequences could be catastrophic. After nine years as a head of year and now as somebody who leads the safeguarding provision and strategy in my school, I want to reassure budding and current heads of year that safeguarding is not as scary as it might seem.

Effective and open communication is fundamental if you are going to be successful with the safeguarding, welfare and wellbeing of the students in your year group. Initially, this is likely to be more about you asking questions and finding out about welfare through experience. Do not be afraid to ask questions and ask your senior leaders to give their own ideas and support where you are unsure. It is potentially dangerous to think that you have all the answers and solutions when it comes to safeguarding young people. Your school will have a designated safeguarding lead and a deputy and these are the people who must be informed of a concern. Never ever hold the risk yourself; you need to trust the experience of colleagues and ensure that you always follow the set procedures and policies that are written for your school.

The balance of being an inexperienced head of year who asks plenty of questions means that, as you progress within your role, you will be seen by your colleagues as an open leader. This will likely lead to you being perceived as approachable and others will seek you out in times of concern and conflict to seek your advice and wisdom, which you will have developed over time. I grew in confidence in my time as a head of year as my experience widened, leading to more trust and better impact with the team of tutors I managed. All of this experience allowed me to develop my affiliative and coaching style of leadership that brings out the best in others.

I found as a head of year that it was important to have regular and strong links with the safeguarding leads in the schools that I worked in. By having weekly informal catch-ups, I was able to be comfortable that actions were taking place to support a young person, even if I didn't know what all of these actions were. I would strongly encourage all heads of year to meet with senior pastoral leaders regularly to talk through key children and current actions being taken to support them. Too often, it can feel as a head of year that you are not being communicated with. To leave this unchallenged could mean that you are not fulfilling your safeguarding responsibility to challenge when appropriate. Excellent communication is at the heart of a strong school culture, where great leaders at all levels appreciate and embrace challenge.

In summary:

- Know your school policy and procedures for child protection and safeguarding, keeping these key documents close at hand. Refer to them regularly as they need to be followed.

- Do not be afraid to ask questions to build your experience with safeguarding and welfare. Remember that understanding this aspect of the head of year role takes time.
- Communicate effectively but sensitively with the full range of colleagues who work with you and the students in your year group.

# Chapter 10 takeaway

## Key points

- As head of year, you may be the best placed person to make a decision about whether a concern crosses over into a safeguarding situation, due to the intelligence and contextual information that you hold on that student. Be prepared to take advice from your designated safeguarding lead if you are not sure, rather than making a decision in isolation.
- Don't be drawn into making knee-jerk reactions based on emotional members of staff. Take your time to assess all of the facts and build up a jigsaw puzzle before you make any significant decisions. When it comes to safeguarding and student welfare, objective decisions are essential.
- Make sure you know your safeguarding responsibilities inside out, so that you can give support and advice to other teachers and support staff in your team if and when they require it. Think about the person you needed when you were just starting out in the profession as a young teacher or tutor. Be that person for them.

## Next steps

- **Read**

  Make sure you have read and understood the 2019a Department for Education statutory guidance 'Keeping children safe in education', paying particular attention to not only the responsibilities of all teachers in the school, but where your role as head of year might be pivotal.

- **Connect**

  Speak to your designated safeguarding lead to plug any gaps you may have on your role as a head of year in the safeguarding process, but also about how much they should expect from you when you refer a case on to them.

- **Reflect**

  Reflect on your previous experience of being an inexperienced member of staff who required advice and support from their head of year. Now you are that person, what support can you offer your colleagues that you may have needed when you were less experienced?

# 11

# Closing the gap

---

**CHAPTER OVERVIEW**

In this chapter we will look at:

- why we need to close the gap
- what gaps there are
- different subgroups of students.

---

## Performance gaps

It wasn't that long ago in education that 'closing the gap' would have meant putting some sealant around the old window frame in your classroom to stop the wind rattling through. However, with the help of Building Schools for the Future (BSF) and a far greater scrutiny on performance data of subgroups, this phrase now means a different thing altogether. As you will be only too well aware, schools are now judged not only on their headline performance measures for attainment, progress, attendance, exclusions and a whole host of other measures, but also on any significantly wide gaps in performance between subgroups of students in any one of those measures. Being above the national average for progress in English might seem great, but if a closer inspection of the data reveals that your girls are doing 15 per cent better in that measure than the boys, then you've got a problem. Questions will be asked about what you are doing to close that gap.

The cynical ones amongst us will say that the quickest way to close a performance gap is to just concentrate on the underperforming group and forget about the group that are outperforming them. By simple logic, if the higher-performing group stop performing at the same increased rate, then the gap will naturally close. However, that would be neglecting our students and I'm pretty sure that's not what we came into teaching to do. We therefore need to look at far more intelligent ways to begin to close these gaps, so that we begin to help students from all subgroups make the progress that they are capable of. If we truly want to educate our children so they can break through statistical stereotypes and use education to aid social mobility, then closing the gaps has to be a priority in our schools.

## A national problem

Although closing the gap has been a national education priority for well over a decade now, unfortunately, due to the size of the problem and the fact the root causes are usually external factors, schools have struggled to resolve a lot of the issues, even with a significant amount of funding having been thrown at this. In 2017, the Education Policy Institute published a report examining the progress made in closing the gap in attainment between disadvantaged students and their peers over a ten-year period (Andrews et al., 2017). The report identifies that, despite considerable investment and targeted intervention programmes by the government, gaps between disadvantaged students and their peers are closing slowly and inconsistently. The report demonstrates the scale of the problem, with statistics in 2016 showing disadvantaged students on average being 19.3 months behind their peers by the time they took their GCSEs, and persistently disadvantaged students being two full years behind. Hope of this being resolved in the near future is put into stark reality when the report concludes that 'at the current rate of progress it would take a full 50 years to reach an equitable education system where disadvantaged pupils did not fall behind their peers during formal education to age 16'.

## *Head of year role*

As head of year, you sit in one of the most privileged positions in the school when it comes to closing the gap. Your knowledge of individual students, what motivates them and what holds them back is absolutely key to being able to put strategies in place to improve their performance. Blanket strategies for a whole subgroup of students, for example boys or pupil premium students, will rarely work for everyone. Although 'boys' might be a subgroup that is underperforming in English, there will undoubtedly be a number of different reasons why. Granted, there may be some common issues that tend to run across the whole subgroup, but an individual understanding of the background of each child and what makes them tick is essential. Without this knowledge, you may as well just purchase a 'raising boys' achievement' strategy from an external consultant and expect to just plug it in and say goodbye to your gap. As we saw in the previous paragraph, throwing money at the problem has not made any significant difference so far.

## *Raising awareness*

Although your senior leadership team and your data team will probably be doing this already, it's important for you as the head of your year group to be constantly reminding teaching staff about any significant gaps between subgroups in your year group and the importance of trying to close those gaps. Because you are living and breathing it, you may feel that it's second nature to you, but for an NQT, they may not even register that they have some gaps in the data in their class. Their initial focus has probably been to ensure that their lessons are all planned, that their marking is up to date and that they are holding their own in terms of behaviour management. Understanding that they have got a significant gap in performance in their classroom between boys and girls or pupil premium and non-pupil premium students may be the furthest thing from their mind. It is therefore your job to keep banging the drum for your students and to keep reminding the staff who teach your students about any emerging subgroups that are underperforming.

## Personal reflection

Are you able to identify the gaps in performance in your whole-school headline measures from last year?

_____

_____

_____

_____

_____

_____

_____

Looking specifically at your year group, or a specific year group in school, are your gaps similar to the whole-school gaps? Or do you have specific issues that are different to the whole-school picture?

_____

_____

_____

_____

_____

# Understanding the different types of gaps

When thinking about gaps in performance data between subgroups in your school, most people tend to think of the most prominent subgroup – disadvantaged students. This is largely because of the prominence that this subgroup gets, due to the significant extra funding that each student receives per year, in order to try to close that gap (currently £935 per student in 2018–19). However, this is not the only subgroup of students that is tracked by Ofsted and the Department for Education to see whether there are underlying inequalities in your school. Subgroups such as gender, students with special educational needs and disabilities (SEND) and those with English as a second language (EAL) will all be closely monitored in the same way that disadvantaged students are. It is vital that you are aware of this and that your internal tracking systems are picking up any significant subgroups that are showing underperformance against their peers.

## Insignificant groups

Although you will probably have students in all of the subgroups I have mentioned, you need to remember that, depending on your school context, some of those subgroups may be insignificant due to the number of students that make up that group. For example, if you only have a very small proportion of EAL students in your school, then the performance of the group can significantly change depending on only one or two students. If you suddenly get a couple of students classed as EAL who do particularly well in a certain performance measure, it wouldn't be reliable to present that data alongside your headline measures and suggest that you've done some great work in closing the gap between EAL students and non-EAL students. Any Ofsted inspector worth their salt won't look at that data until the group becomes 'statistically significant' based on the number of students in your school. In mathematical terms, any group size less than ten per cent of your population is open to significant fluctuation and volatility.

## Numerical context

One way of helping to judge how statistically significant a group is, or to see past the spreadsheets and look at the real size of the problem on your hands, is to convert your percentages into numbers of students. A gap of 20 per cent on your spreadsheet or data dashboard might appear to be quite a significant issue on first look and could give an inspector a trail to investigate, but when you realise that 20 per cent is only three students, then it puts the gap into context. On the flip side, this also works as a reminder of how much work you may have to do to close a gap. You may have a large cohort of students with a ten per cent gap that equates to 30 students. Getting 30 students to improve in a short space of time may not be what you want to hear. But if you only look at the percentages, your eyes might be drawn to the 20 per cent gap and not the ten per cent gap, meaning you may miss the real issue.

## *Performance data*

Once you have established which groups of students are statistically significant, you then need to look at all of the key performance indicators to see where any gaps may have opened. In my experience of both school leadership and working as a head of year, the following areas are the key performance indicators that are most commonly analysed within student subgroups to determine whether there are any performance gaps:

- **Student outcomes** – attainment, progress, external examination results.

- **Behaviour** – internal behaviour tracking data, inclusion sanctions, fixed-term exclusion data.

- **Attendance** – punctuality, absence, persistently absent students.

Regular analysis of these data sets is extremely important if you want to be working hard to eliminate any inequalities in student performance. It's one thing to have your data team know all the statistics and be able to print colourful graphs for every data entry, but as a head of year you need to put numbers to the percentages and then names to the numbers.

# Subgroups

Although every school is different and context is always key, here are some common subgroups that may be statistically significant in your school and where you may be already trying to close a specific performance gap.

## Disadvantaged students

The educational performance of students from disadvantaged backgrounds is (on average across the country) much lower than that of their more affluent peers. Recognising the need to improve the performance of disadvantaged students, the government introduced the pupil premium in 2011, directing specific funding to help close this gap. According to the January 2018 national statistics (Department for Education, 2018b), disadvantaged students made up 13.3 per cent of all students in state-funded secondary schools (12 per cent in academies), but this rises to 38.7 per cent of the population in special schools and 39 per cent in pupil referral units. Disadvantage also has a big influence on students' life chances. As the Social Mobility and Child Poverty Commission's 2014 'State of the nation' report highlights, students from disadvantaged backgrounds are 'twice as likely to be not in education, employment or training (NEET) at age 16' (p. 64) and at higher risk of ending up in poverty as adults. The correlation is quite startling when you look at exclusion figures. In 2016–17, there were twice as many disadvantaged students (Ever 6) permanently excluded from secondary schools compared to their peers.

## Gender split

In terms of gender, girls still significantly outperform boys when it comes to attainment, although recent GCSE reform to examinations has narrowed the gap ever so slightly. In 2018 girls outperformed boys by nine per cent at the 9–5 threshold and then by six per cent when looking at students attaining grade

7 and above. The gap is even more pronounced when you look at behaviour and exclusion figures. Even though the population of boys and girls is pretty even in UK secondary schools (with 1.4 million boys and 1.3 million girls in 2018 according to national statistics; Department for Education, 2018b), boys are nearly three times more likely to be fixed term excluded and four times more likely to be permanently excluded than girls. Having 'boy-heavy' year groups may be quite significant when it comes to looking at school performance, so it's vital that you understand your cohort.

## Special educational needs and disabilities

Some students may require more help to learn and develop than children of the same age. If this is the case they may be classed as having special educational needs so they can get extra support. However, even with this extra support, school performance indicators show that students with special educational needs (SEN) are still significantly outperformed by their peers. On average, the attainment 8 score for students with SEN in 2016–17 was 27.2 compared to 49.8 for those with no SEN. The progress 8 score for students with SEN was –0.61 compared to 0.08 for those with no SEN. This indicates that students with SEN achieve on average around half a grade lower per subject than other students with the same Key Stage 2 attainment. This increases to over a grade less progress per subject for students with a statement of SEN or an education health care plan (Department for Education, 2019b).

## Ethnic groups

Depending on your school context and where your school is situated, you may have a significantly larger or smaller proportion of students with English as an additional language (EAL) than other schools. Statistics from The Bell Foundation (2015) show us that almost a quarter of schools in the UK (22 per cent) have less than one per cent EAL students, but in 8.4 per cent of schools, EAL students constitute over half the school population. When it comes to examination performance, EAL students catch up with their peers by the age of 16 on average: 'At age 5, only 44% of EAL students have achieved a good level of development compared to 54% of other students. By age 16, this gap has narrowed significantly with 58.3% achieving five A*–C [9–5] GCSEs including English and maths compared to 60.9% of other pupils.' However, what these averages don't show is that results differ vastly when we look at specific groups of EAL students. Students who speak Portuguese, Somali, Lingala and Lithuanian, for example, have particularly low outcomes at the age of 16, whereas those who speak Russian and Spanish do especially well.

## Personal reflection

How well do you know the current cohort of students in your year group and the proportion of students who fall into significant subgroups?

_____

_____

_____

_____

_____

How are these subgroups performing against national statistics? Are they broadly in line with the national picture that we have discussed or are some of your subgroups bucking the trend? If so, what are you doing with them that is making a difference?

_____

_____

_____

_____

_____

# Utilising your team to close the gap

Closing the gap cannot just be a one-person job; it is far bigger than that. Mark Allen reflects on how he has strategically closed the attendance gap in his school by working with a cross section of leaders across the whole school.

## PROFESSIONAL PERSPECTIVE: CLOSING THE ATTENDANCE GAP

### By Mark Allen, Former Vice Principal at Astrea Academy Dearne, now Trust Senior Vice Principal at Maltby Academy, Maltby

I started my leadership journey as a head of year and it made me realise how much I loved the pastoral part of school life and what an important job I had. The role enabled me to develop the expertise and experience that I now rely heavily on in my role as Senior Vice Principal.

As a head of year in the current political climate, the one group you will be asked about the most and where you will have to indicate financial acumen is the 'disadvantaged' group. It is crucial to show how you spend the money you receive to support this cohort to close the gap between them and their peers. At Astrea Academy Dearne, 53 per cent of our cohort were classed as 'disadvantaged'. This required our heads of year to have oversight of over 100 disadvantaged students per year group.

The importance of this group was indicated when an Ofsted monitoring visit in 2017 highlighted that the attendance gap between our disadvantaged cohort and others was too wide and we needed to improve their attendance. The attendance of our disadvantaged students was three per cent lower than that of their peers. It was my job as pupil premium and pastoral lead to work on closing this gap. I knew I couldn't do this alone and needed the help, knowledge and skills of my team of heads of year.

A head of year can have a huge positive influence on their year group and their families. Regular communication is key and, if this is coupled with clear, positive messages about your ethos and school culture, you can close any gap. As Vice Principal and strategic lead of attendance, I utilised the knowledge and skillset of my heads of year to close this gap as a team. Our strategy involved small but significant systems that impacted weekly on the attendance of disadvantaged children. Each head of year analysed their cohort's data and chose ten to 15 students (all disadvantaged) to meet with, monitor and liaise with parents. Each cohort included students just below or just above the persistently absent figure of 90 per cent. Every week our heads of year set appropriate targets and used the following strategies to ensure their students attended school:

- phone calls
- home visits
- attendance passports

- weekly certificates for 100 per cent attendance
- bacon butty and tea or coffee review days
- postcards home.

As a head of year, it is important to remember that you are a leader of a powerful team of people. Our heads of year also made it a requirement that every form tutor tracked ten disadvantaged students in their form. The tutors developed a signing-in system, created attendance displays, made phone calls home and designed their own reward system too. This meant each week between 80 and 100 of our disadvantaged cohort were being tracked by a leader in school.

Heads of year can give powerful messages each week in assembly time and our team utilised this time to celebrate individual successes with certificates and prizes. They also had form group versus form group competitions and we tied attendance into our house competition too. Every half term we would have an attendance competition across the school, with the winning year group getting rewards such as an ice cream van, roller blading disco, cinema experience and more.

Think what messages you could deliver. How would you do this? What mechanisms do you have to display attendance? How would you fund it? What awards or rewards would you give? How would you get student voice on this?

As a middle leader in school, you can tap into the work of other colleagues, therefore creating a school-wide strategic approach. Colleagues such as the reception or main office team, designated safeguarding lead, educational welfare officer, data team, senior leadership team, pupil premium champion or lead, rewards TLR holder and SENCO can all be utilised effectively to help you close that gap.

Our joined-up approach increased the attendance of disadvantaged students by 0.44 per cent. Considering that over 50 per cent of all students fall into this cohort, an increase of this nature in attendance indicates a significant impact. This work also meant that we closed the attendance gap for disadvantaged students by 0.39 per cent. The improved attendance of our disadvantaged cohort also helped in contributing to closing the progress gap at Astrea Academy Dearne in our 2018 outcomes.

My advice on closing any gap would be to remember the following:

- You are not on your own – utilise your team of tutors.
- Strategically join up with other leaders in your setting – we all want every child to succeed and all leaders will have groups to focus on.
- Use your pupil premium champion's knowledge and ask for some of their funding to support your work.
- Work with external partners to close the gap.
- Communicate regularly with parents and carers.
- Embrace your ethos and culture to deliver your message.
- Drive your strategy, immerse yourself in it and regularly review your impact.

## Chapter 11 takeaway

### Key points

- Gaps in performance between different groups of students are a national problem, but something that schools are held to account over closing. Simply being above the national average is not good enough anymore if you have significant gaps between subgroups of students.
- It is not only attainment data where gaps in performance are scrutinised. Attendance, behaviour and exclusion

figures are also important to work on when looking to close the gaps in your key performance indicators.

- Depending on the context of your school, you will have different proportions of students in different subgroups. However, these will only become significant subgroups if they contain approximately ten per cent of your student population.

## Next steps

- **Read**

  Read *Narrowing the Attainment Gap* by Daniel Sobel. This book explores the real reasons behind the attainment gap, providing guidance and ready-to-use templates to help drive school improvement and the closing of achievement gaps.

- **Connect**

  Speak to your data team to get a detailed breakdown of all of the subgroups in your year group, together with an analysis of their performance in key school measures against their peers.

- **Reflect**

  Reflect on your knowledge of students in each of these subgroups. What is holding them back from achieving in line with their peers? What can you do to remove these barriers?

# 12

# Engaging with parents

---

**CHAPTER OVERVIEW**

In this chapter we will look at:

- working in partnership with parents to raise achievement
- barriers to engagement
- different forms of communication.

---

## Working in partnership with parents to raise achievement

With the focus of our attentions on the students in front of us every day, we can sometimes forget that the parents of our students can play an equally significant part in raising achievement. Without parental support, many of the strategies and initiatives that we put in place can be either undone at home or not supported sufficiently to have any significant impact. The perfect conditions for rapid and sustained improvement in either a group of students or an individual is where the conditions at school and at home are consistent and mutually supportive in raising achievement. If one side is contradicting the other, or one is not supportive of what the other is trying to achieve, then students can quite easily play one off against the other. Effective home–school partnerships are therefore key in any high-performing school. This requires communication though. How do parents know what we expect of them in terms of supporting their children if we do not communicate this with them? And how do we know that they are being deliberately unsupportive? It may just be that they aren't clear on how to support their child effectively and, if we showed them, they'd be more than happy to replicate those conditions at home.

## *Empathy*

When entering into any partnership with a parent, it's vital to have parental empathy for them. It's fine to have high standards and aspirations for what we'd like to see away from school, but we need to put ourselves in the shoes of parents to truly empathise with them. Do you know what it's like to try to get two children to do two hours of homework after they have been at school for a whole day? And do you really want to battle with your children over this in the little time you have with them between coming in from work and them going to bed? The parents amongst us will probably recognise both of these scenarios, but how many of us forget this when we come to speaking with parents? A little empathy in these situations will go a long way to building trust and strong relationships with the parents of your students. Being able to bring your experience as a parent to certain situations gives you far more authenticity because you can relate to their experiences, frustrations and problems. However, even without being a parent, you can still put yourselves in the shoes of a parent and think about how they may be feeling. Thinking like a parent when dealing with parents will always mean you are looking at the bigger picture and not just what it means for you in your office.

## *Being supportive*

I remember as an inexperienced and young head of year being worried and nervous about having to deal with parents. I used to feel that they would be coming into school to defend their child at all times and disagree with any sanctions or interventions that we put in place. However, throughout my 15 years of experience in pastoral roles, I've found that most parents just want to support their child, in whichever ways they can, to reach their potential. Although they may not initially show it in the most obvious ways, parents are usually happy to support the school if they can clearly see that it will have a positive impact on their child. As long as we have a clear understanding of the rules in any given situation, then people who are fair and firm in their actions and judgements usually get our support. The problem arises when decisions are taken that we don't seem to understand, or we feel that somebody has been treated unfairly, based on our previous experiences or knowledge. Taking the time to communicate your expectations to begin with and then explain any decisions to parents, together with an underlying message that this is always to support their child to achieve, should stand you in good stead.

# Barriers to engagement

Although, like me, you may find that most parents are supportive, every school will have parents who are harder to reach and are not engaging with school. As head of year, it is your job to identify their individual barriers to engagement and work with them to remove them, so that they can support the school and their child in reaching their potential. From my experience, here are some of the most common barriers to parental engagement.

## Poor school experience as a child

Just like the dentist, if you've had bad memories of school as a child, you'll probably be carrying preconceptions of what it's going to be like as an adult. Similarly, if you've had negative experiences of a hospital, it's not a place that fills you with warmth and happiness if you have to go there again. This is crucial to understand as a head of year because there may be a large proportion of your parents who had negative experiences at school and will be judging you on that basis before they've even met you. One negative experience of a teacher, a head of year or a headteacher means, for some parents, that we're all going to be the same. Turning these preconceived ideas around into positive experiences can be hard but is not impossible. Demonstrating to parents how the schools of today are very different to the days of *Grange Hill* may be necessary for some. Constantly reiterating that we are doing everything possible to support their child in achieving will be a message that you'll need to reinforce with many.

## Poor experience at your school

From time to time, some parents may have experienced a poor situation at your own school. This may be the way a situation has been handled, a lack of communication, or a general poor standard of education or care from either a teacher or another leader. Understanding and appreciating this is vital if you are going to try to turn this relationship around into a positive one. You may not be able to do anything about what has happened previously, but you can certainly do something about their experience of the care in your school going forward. In some cases, this may even give you a better platform from which to build a strong relationship. If a parent can see that you are operating with far more empathy, skill and proficiency than they have previously experienced, then you'll become their favourite 'go to' person in the school.

## Language and cultural barriers

Depending on your school context, some parents may want to be extremely supportive but, due to language barriers, they may not be able to converse effectively with you on the telephone or in meetings, thus reducing the effectiveness of their support due to a lack of knowledge and understanding of certain situations. Put yourself in the shoes of a parent who has just arrived in the country and speaks very little English. You may want to do everything you can to support your child and the school, but if you cannot effectively communicate with the school, you'll find it extremely difficult to do the little things that we take for granted. Simple tasks such as ringing the school to explain an absence or writing a note in your child's planner about a missing piece of homework suddenly become quite challenging, but can look from the outside like a parent who is unsupportive. Working with your in-school or local authority support team to ensure that these families are supported is essential. There are also many easy-to-use digital translation solutions that you can use with families to translate letters and key school information and even assist with face-to-face conversations (search for Microsoft Learning Tools and Google Translate for more information).

## Work

For some families, their own work commitments can get in the way of them engaging in school life. Working in environments where they can't take phone calls throughout the school day and can't leave work to attend school meetings can cause problems when it comes to responsive parenting. This does not mean to say that they are not being supportive, but it may just be a barrier that you need to appreciate and work around. Parents who undertake shift work also experience these barriers from time to time. It may be that they can take a call from you throughout the day but can never attend a parents' evening because their line of work means that evening or nights are when they are at work. Finding alternative arrangements and times to effectively communicate with these parents is really important and will be appreciated by these parents in the long run. Simply accepting that a parent can never come into school when it suits you, and therefore not trying to keep the lines of communication open, means that your inflexible nature will be another barrier to that student achieving their true potential.

## Personal reflection

How effectively have you built up partnerships with the parents in your year group? Are there any parents with whom you need to work on this? If so, how will you do this?

_____

_____

_____

_____

_____

_____

_____

Thinking about the common barriers to engagement, which barriers are most common in your year group or school and what can you do to break them down?

_____

_____

_____

_____

_____

# Different forms of communication

There are many ways in which we can communicate with the parents in our school, especially in this age of innovative and digital communication. However, not all digital communication is effective for every situation. My experience has shown me that one method can be more effective for certain situations than others. Choosing the right medium is crucial if you want to effectively communicate with your parents. Let's take a look at the most common forms of communication that we use in school and how we might want to use each one for certain situations with parents.

## *Phone call*

This is probably by far the most common form of communication that a head of year uses when communicating with parents. It's great for quick or urgent contact with parents when you want to talk about a situation in depth, explaining what has happened and why. A phone call is far more human than the majority of other forms of communication because you can connect with someone, have a proper conversation with them and hear both sides of any story. Getting the chance to speak to a parent and demonstrate your parental empathy also helps to build up strong, lasting relationships. Phone calls are also great for regularly keeping parents informed about how their child is doing. If we keep parents in the loop throughout the year, they can hopefully support us with all the little things before they get to be big things. Nobody wants to first hear about a situation when it becomes really serious, especially if you tell them that it's been brewing for a few weeks. Most parents will tell you that if they had known about an issue earlier on, they could have done something about it.

## Text message

Text messages are by far the most informal type of communication but also the quickest. Text messages should only really be used as quick reminders about dates or events, or when you are sending bulk messages of this nature to the whole year group. Important information relating to a specific student should be relayed in other ways. Most schools now have systems to send text messages to parents, but most of these systems are only designed for one-way communication, meaning that parents can't respond to them directly. This tends to annoy parents if they want to respond, because it cannot be instant like in a conversation. Instead it would mean that a parent would have to contact the school by phone and not necessarily get to speak to you.

## Email

Probably the most underused form of communication with parents is email. With the best will in the world, you cannot always guarantee that you will speak to a parent when you call them. Work commitments mean that some parents are uncontactable throughout the day. Email can bridge the gap between text messages and phone calls. An email can be long enough to include the whole detail and can also facilitate a conversation by directly replying to the sender. Email can also be used out of school hours if you so choose. A distressed parent may email you on an evening and all it might take is a quick reply to say that you've received their concern and that you'll be onto it first thing in the morning to put their mind at rest. The other benefit of email is that it can all be tracked and traced as evidence of what you've said or not said in any given conversation.

## Formal letter

The clue is in the title here. 'Formal' letters on school-headed paper are great for formal reasons, such as exclusions, school reports, attendance issues and so on. If the first time that you are reporting a minor concern to a parent you write to them formally, you'll give them a huge shock and you can be sure they'll not be very happy about it. Save this form of communication for when you really need to convey the significance of your message, be that positive or negative.

## Parental meetings

Unless a parent just walks into reception demanding to speak to someone, parental meetings are usually scheduled on the back of having some form of previous communication with them. In my experience, this is when you've been communicating with a parent quite regularly about a certain issue but there's been no improvement in school, so a meeting has been arranged to talk about the situation in more detail. Depending on the specific nature of the situation, you may want to speak to the parent alone, or invite the student to join you as well. There will also be times where the parent is the one who requests the meeting. This may be due to a level of dissatisfaction from the parent, or where they need our support. In these instances, it is important to try to be as accommodating as possible, without just dropping everything because someone is demanding to see you this very minute.

## *Parents' evenings*

Usually scheduled once per year, parents' evenings are a chance for parents to speak directly to the teachers who teach their child and receive accurate information about their performance in that subject. As head of year on that evening, it is your responsibility to support the teachers, especially if you know there will be some difficult conversations or potential flash points. A detailed knowledge of your year group and any strained relationships between parents and teachers will allow you to know where you need to provide some support. This may be especially important for inexperienced teachers or NQTs. You may decide on the evening that you also want to meet certain parents you may have been communicating regularly with over the phone. Meeting face to face hopefully allows you to build stronger relationships and let parents see you as a real person who cares about their child.

## *Responding to communication*

As a head of year new to the role, I always remember some advice I was given about responding to communication. My headteacher at the time told me that, as a general rule of thumb, you should respond using the same form of communication.

For example, responding to a telephone message by writing to them isn't appropriate. Likewise, if someone has written formally to the school to complain, then it deserves a formal written response, not just a text message.

## *Being proactive*

Whichever form of communication you choose to use, make sure that you are proactive with it. If you've been texting home or calling parents for positive reasons since the start of the year, then when it comes to making a phone call regarding a concern about a student, you can never be accused of only contacting home for negative reasons. There are also times when a situation has occurred in school and you know that the student in question will be going home to tell their parents a very different side of the story. However difficult the conversation might be, and however much you're not looking forward to making that phone call, if you get to the parent first and give your side of events, it will be far easier. Trying to make a difficult phone call when the parent is already loaded with ammunition from their child is not a conversation that you'll enjoy.

### **Personal reflection**

Which forms of communication do you use with parents and for what reasons?

_____

_____

_____

_____

_____

Are there any forms of communication that we have discussed that you could utilise more effectively?

_____

_____

_____

_____

_____

# Record-keeping

With the amount of communicating that a head of year does every day with parents, it is vital that you keep accurate records of conversations you have had, for your benefit and that of the wider staff. Vikki Fawcett reflects on why this is important and how this helps to build positive relationships with the parents in your year group.

## PROFESSIONAL PERSPECTIVE: RECORD-KEEPING IS ESSENTIAL IN MAINTAINING POSITIVE RELATIONSHIPS WITH PARENTS

### By Vikki Fawcett, Head of Learning at Woodham Academy, Newton Aycliffe

Having now had the privilege of being a head of year (or head of learning, as the role is known in my school) for ten years, it is useful to reflect on how things have changed. As a new head of year, I can remember being overwhelmed with the amount of information I was expected to store and remember. Juggling a job as an English teacher, with the planning, marking and actual teaching, there was surely no more capacity to include anything else. Prioritising and time management are therefore essential to being successful as a head of year. My advice is simple: record everything, then it cannot be questioned. Gone are the days of writing everything in a diary; we now have access to excellent recording systems that make communication with parents much more efficient. Recording everything may seem, at first, an impossible and time-consuming task but I assure you, it is worth it. If it becomes part of your everyday working life, you will soon realise effective record-keeping saves time rather than wastes it.

Communication, with parents especially, ensures a successful environment for a child to achieve their potential; this is after all a teacher's, head of year's and parent's main priority. You need to work as a team. Positive relationships with parents are cemented when they know you have their child's best interests at heart and that you care as much as they do about their child's success. If you can explain to a parent exactly what has happened in a situation and the support their child has received and can confirm all contact so far, with dates and often times, you can be sure that most communication (even when it has not started off positively) will be successful. Every incident of positive contact with parents helps to secure conducive working relationships and achieves the best results for a child.

Unfortunately, not all communication starts off in a positive way. As a head of year, you find yourself dealing with difficult situations and conversations often. Potentially troublesome conversations should always be dealt with face to face where possible. A parent always appreciates it when they can put a face to a name; it supports empathy from both sides and gives a human perspective to a situation. The best way to deal with the 'bad days' that you will inevitably have as a head of year is to finish every day with a positive. I always find time to make a positive phone call in these instances. Ending your day with positive communication with parents not only secures good relationships between yourself and the parent, but it also brings a balance to what can sometimes be a difficult role. As a parent, you appreciate being contacted for praise and this makes the negatives (if there ever are any) much easier to deal with.

To secure positive relationships with parents, always remember:

1 Record everything. Find a recording system that works for you. The best ones can be shared easily with all parties in a situation: professionals, parents and children. (We use CPOMS).
2 Find time to do what is important and do what is most important first.
3 Reflect in a positive way on every incident of contact with parents. Try to remember in the end you both want the same thing – for the child to be successful.
4 End every day on a positive.

## Chapter 12 takeaway

### Key points

- Building a strong partnership with the parents in your year group will help raise achievement. Without their support, the strategies and interventions that you put in place in school will only go so far.
- There are many reasons why parents may not be as engaged as other parents. This is not always down to conscious disengagement, but may be due to other factors preventing them from either understanding your messages or being able to be around during the school day.

- Communication with parents can take many forms. It is vital to pick the right medium of communication for the specific issue that you are dealing with or the message that you are wanting to convey.

## Next steps

- **Read**

  Read Chapter 5 of *Leading on Pastoral Care* by Daniel Sobel, which discusses in detail how to get the very best out of working with parents.

- **Connect**

  Speak to the parents in your year group regularly and proactively to build up lasting positive relationships where you can demonstrate your parental empathy and care for their child.

- **Reflect**

  Reflect on how you have been using the various forms of communication previously. Are there ways that you can communicate more effectively?

# 13

# Leading assemblies

---

## CHAPTER OVERVIEW

In this chapter we will look at:

- the importance of assemblies
- consistent assembly structures and routines
- themes for assemblies.

---

# The importance of assemblies

Assemblies usually happen every day in our schools, with heads of year typically taking responsibility for leading them for the students in their year group. They can take place in specific assembly halls, sports halls or dining halls or even be live-streamed into classrooms depending on the time of year and the context of the school. However, far too often assemblies are just seen as an opportunity for a head of year to give out messages to students and quickly just become an information-giving session, whether it be positive or negative messages, without any type of strategic direction or thought. The best schools use this time wisely and strategically plan the precious time they have in front of their whole year group, so that they make the most of it.

## *Sense of community*

The first thing to be noted about the importance of school assemblies is the fact that they are one of the only times that you get to bring a whole year group together. This creates a strong sense of community amongst the students and your staff, helping them to feel that they are all part of something bigger than just their class. The bigger your school, the more challenging this might be depending on the facilities you have available to you, but it should not be underestimated how important this collective gathering is to community spirit. Not only does it give you the opportunity to personally address your students every time you come together, but it is also an opportunity to deliver the same key messages to the tutors and staff in the room. A teacher's wider role in education is to nurture and develop our young people outside of our expert subject domains. Getting staff to attend assemblies, even if they are not a form tutor, is a great way of reminding them of this.

From time to time, facilities can become an issue. The most common problem for assemblies is around the examination season, where main halls, sports halls and any other large spaces are usually set up for exams, meaning that it becomes increasingly difficult to find a suitable venue to hold a year group assembly. The easiest thing to do is to postpone assemblies until the exams are over, but this could be nearly two months. Do you really want to relinquish your opportunity to bring your year group together for this length of time? I have experienced first-hand instances of increased negative behaviour across a year group that can be attributed to the cancelling of assemblies for such a long period of time, giving students no focal point or sense of belonging to the wider school community. When our usual facilities are not available, we must be far more creative in our approaches to assemblies, rather than just taking the easy option and cancelling them. With advances in modern technology, you can easily live-stream an assembly or key message to all of the classes in the school without having to physically bring people together.

## *Values and ethos*

Every school will claim to have a mission statement, a set of values and a strong ethos about how they want their students to turn out after five years in their care. You can usually find these proudly displayed on their school website and on signs in the school car park or on the side of the building itself. Without these key messages and values being driven from the front by the head of year or a senior leader in the form of weekly assemblies when the whole year group gathers together, it can be quite a challenge for individual subject teachers to weave these messages into the curriculum that they deliver. With exam specifications already written for them and teachers constantly complaining of too much content and too little time to deliver it, the need for a formal collective gathering of the year group every week is even more important.

Not only does it allow for a figurehead in the school to constantly weave these key messages into the minds of our young people, but it also enables us to remind students of the strict standards that we expect in our school and that, like everyone else in that assembly, they are going to be treated equally and fairly. The formality of an assembly with all students following the same rules as each other is a great way to practically demonstrate to young people the need for a collective understanding and tolerance of rules. For some students, this sense of formality may be the only experience they have had in their lives, so the importance of instilling strong core values in this way could be vitally important in your quest to develop well-rounded and educated young people.

## *Collective worship*

School assembly time also serves to promote opportunities for acts of collective worship. Under the Education Act 1996, all maintained schools, except maintained special schools, must provide daily collective worship for all registered students. This has now also been extended to include the new academy landscape of UK schools, with the Department for Education publishing information for academies and free schools in 2013 about providing religious education (RE) and collective worship. The guidance states that:

> 'An academy's funding agreement is drafted to mirror the requirements for acts of collective worship in maintained schools. Each pupil must take part in a daily act of collective worship unless they have been withdrawn by their parents, or if in the sixth form they have decided to withdraw themselves. This applies to academies with and without a religious designation.'

Although this may seem quite a challenge for most schools to bring their students together every day for an act of collective worship, it is up to each and every school to decide how this is carried out. Although the guidance explains that collective worship in schools without a designated religious character will be 'wholly or mainly of a broadly Christian nature', many schools have widened the approach of their collective worship to focus on the spiritual, moral, social and cultural development of our children. Halton Borough Council's (2017) guidelines for collective worship explains that elements of collective worship could include:

- developing a sense of awe and wonder about the world
- affirming positive values, such as honesty or self-sacrifice
- encouraging responsibility for making personal decisions
- celebrating achievement and special occasions.

## Personal reflection

When your usual facilities are not available for your assembly, how could you still conduct an assembly, rather than relinquishing your opportunity to speak to your whole year group?

_____

_____

_____

_____

_____

_____

What are your current provisions for meeting the Department for Education guidance on providing opportunities for an act of collective worship for your students?

_____

_____

_____

_____

_____

_____

# Consistent assembly structures and routines

As we have discussed already in this chapter, an assembly helps to reinforce the formality of school and enables you to model the standards that you want for the students in your year group. Whether it's smart uniform, punctuality or just the ability to walk in and out of the assembly hall in silence, the formal nature of an assembly is a perfect way to promote your core messages. Great schools deliberately and strategically use their assemblies to reinforce key themes and messages by having them consistently displayed or mentioned to students as part of the normal structure of an assembly. Just like the routine of a classroom environment, there may be some fundamental topics and themes that you want to discuss or highlight with students every time you come together as a year group. This can be either as part of or as an extension to the spiritual, moral, social and cultural aspects of your assembly. This may come in the shape of student rewards or positive reinforcement of attendance and punctuality. Either way, whatever you choose to prioritise will soon be perceived as being important to the students in your year group if it becomes a permanent fixture in your assemblies.

## *Planning*

If you want your assemblies to have an impact (and why shouldn't you?), then you need to put the same time and effort into the planning of them as you would do for your classroom teaching. After all, your classroom teaching only has an impact on 30 students at a time. An assembly has the potential to impact a whole year group, which in some schools could be up to 300 students. Not only should you plan the obvious features like the content or theme of an assembly, which we will discuss on page 218, but you should also spend time thinking about the consistent structure of your assemblies so that you can include all of the key areas and messages that you want to prioritise. Rather than just turning up every week and talking to the students about whatever has been annoying you with your year group, it may be wise to think strategically about what you need to include as part of your assembly routine.

Every year group in every school will be different to another year group, so you may need to tweak and change your approach slightly depending on the cohort you are leading. You may have some whole-school priorities that you want to cover as part of your routines, but there may also be some year-group-specific data that informs some of your key messages. You may have a year group who require a constant reminder about punctuality, or a year group who need to know that it is okay to be rewarded in front of their peers. This information and intelligence you have about your year group is vital to ensure that your assemblies not only allow for collective worship, but also help you improve the outcomes on any one of the multiple performance indicators that we are held to account for. Assemblies planned without this prior knowledge of the year group in mind are just an 'off the shelf' event that has limited impact on the students who are sat there.

## *Consistency*

Although each year group will have slight differences to the content and key messages in their assemblies, it is wise for schools to try to ensure consistency of approach between each year group's assembly structures. Granted there will be significant differences to the content of a Year 7 assembly when compared to a Year 11 assembly, but the routines of how students line up, how they enter the hall and how they are expected to behave, participate and respond should be similar in expectation. This 'house style' is a strategy employed frequently by schools in the classroom, with senior leaders wanting students to experience classroom consistency, but more often than not they leave the head of year in charge of how they plan and deliver their assemblies. More effective whole-school structures to pastoral leadership have specific structures in place that help support the individual heads of year in planning their assemblies, knowing that what they are delivering and how they are delivering it is helping the bigger picture of school improvement.

A school-wide consistent approach to assemblies also helps students when there is a change of head of year. In some schools certain heads of year stay where they are at the end of the year (this is particularly common for those leading Year 7 and Year 11) and the students move on to the next head of year. In other circumstances, heads of year will naturally gain promotion to other roles and students may have several figureheads in the year group throughout their time at school. However, irrespective of the person stood at the front of the assembly, whether that be a new or existing head of year, an assistant, a senior leader or the headteacher, a consistent approach to the nature and delivery of the assemblies will make them far more successful and impactful due to the specific 'house style' that has been carefully and strategically thought about.

## *Negative messages*

Without any strategic prior planning or house style, assemblies can very quickly turn into an opportunity for a head of year to constantly deliver negative messages about issues like bad behaviour that may only apply to a small percentage of the audience. This need to 'get things off our chest' comes when there has been a series of incidents in the days leading up to an assembly, so the natural way to want to resolve it is to address these issues head on with the whole year group. Now there is no issue in doing this from time to time where necessary (as we've already discussed, if you highlight it in your assembly, then you are demonstrating how important it is), but it needs to be done sparingly. If your students always hear you doing this in your assemblies, then it will quickly lose any effect. Like a teacher who shouts all of the time, you suddenly lose the ability to make an impression by raising your voice because it's just the norm.

Think also about the number of students that you are addressing in your assembly. Have they all been badly behaved or late for school this week? Put yourselves in their shoes for a minute. Imagine doing everything that was asked of you (and more) every day and then having someone come and tell you all off in a really bad mood because a small proportion of people had not followed the rules. I guess you would be pretty annoyed and it wouldn't give you a great impression of the person speaking to you. Negative messages delivered in this way are also usually very ineffective because it's easy to think as a student that the message is not aimed directly at you. Collective ownership of a problem is much easier to let slide off your shoulders than individual responsibility for something. We must try to avoid slipping into this mode as much as possible as it is a poor way to regularly use the quality time you have to speak to the fantastic students in your year group.

### Personal reflection

Does your school have a consistent approach to the delivery of assemblies? How consistent are you from week to week with your own structure and delivery of key messages?

_____

_____

_____

_____

_____

How often do you feel yourself getting drawn into delivering negative messages to the whole year group via an assembly? Are there better ways in which you can do this?

_____

_____

_____

_____

_____

# Themes for assemblies

If you have followed my advice above and are now thinking about strategically planning the content of your assemblies across the academic year, rather than just in the few days or minutes leading up to an assembly, then you'll be thinking about what themes you can cover. By planning your assemblies this way, you can be sure to hit all of the themes you want across the year, together with avoiding falling into the trap of ranting about something that has frustrated you during the preceding week. In some schools these themes may already have been strategically planned for you, but in others you may have freedom to choose. Either way, having them calendared so that you and your team know what is coming up is good practice.

## Seasonal themes

The changing seasons of the calendar year can help you theme assemblies, bringing the world, the environment and the local community around us into sharper focus. We can probably all remember harvest assemblies when we were younger and the great links that this can build between the school and the local community. This type of assembly is the perfect opportunity to come together as a year group and help people not as fortunate as ourselves.

## Religious festivals

There are many religious festivals throughout the year that can help you promote a diverse and inclusive culture in your school. Aside from the more commonly celebrated festivals in the UK such as Christmas and Easter, there are many more high-profile religious festivals such as Ramadan, Hanukkah and Diwali that can be highlighted or celebrated through seasonal assemblies, helping to educate your students about the diverse world that we live in.

## Charities

Whether your school has an official school charity or not, there are always opportunities to promote national or local charities through school assemblies. High-profile charities such as Children in Need, Comic Relief and Sport Relief are more widely known by students due to the nature of the exposure they receive on television. These charities also have activities and events that you can get involved in as a year group in school. However, just as important are some local charities that might mean more to your students because they can see first-hand the benefit that they have in your community.

## *External speakers*

There are lots of organisations, both locally and nationally, that are probably chomping at the bit to get into schools and speak to students. At various times of the year, you may want to take advantage of this to increase the authenticity and realism of your messages in assembly. Sometimes the same message that you would have delivered coming from a fresh face is all that is needed to drive home the message. Utilising the local police and fire brigade around bonfire night is always useful, together with ex-students from last year's Year 11 who can come back and talk to the current Year 11 about how to apply themselves in the run-up to and throughout the examination season.

# Strategic leadership of assemblies

As we've discussed, the strategic leadership of your assemblies is key if you want them to have a positive impact on your students. Jane Darbyshire reflects on how she has strategically led the delivery of school assemblies, ensuring that certain key themes are a consistent fixture in all year group assemblies.

## PROFESSIONAL PERSPECTIVE: LINKING ASSEMBLIES TO WHOLE-SCHOOL PRIORITIES

### By Jane Darbyshire, Deputy Headteacher, Stokesley School

Assemblies are the cornerstone to successful leadership of your year or house. Throughout my 16 years' experience as a head of year and an assistant headteacher for pastoral care, my personal belief is that assemblies are the most integral part of any successful pastoral system. Assemblies should not just happen; they should be intrinsically linked to whole-school improvement areas, be a focus for tutor time and allow students to consider and reflect upon their own beliefs and morals, as well as delivering consistent, regular messages to promote positive attendance, punctuality and standards of behaviour in line with your school's policies.

Assemblies are your opportunity to nurture and create the whole-school ethos you wish to embed across your year or house. They should also allow you to reward your students in public for the amazing work they demonstrate both in and out of the classroom, creating a culture of success to raise aspirations for all.

Planning your assembly and the schedule for others is key. Requests come from all areas to deliver assemblies, as staff and senior leaders recognise that addressing a whole year group can have huge impact. Poor assemblies are often due to not enough time being given to the planning of the actual assembly itself. This mistake can be catastrophic in damaging the delivery of the message or the launch of a new initiative. As the head of year who is responsible for planning your schedules and delivering assemblies for your year group, you need to be efficient and organised. Liaising with your line manager and other stakeholders needs to be done in advance. Whilst this planning may be your priority, remember that it isn't for others. Set and share appropriate timescales so everyone knows the procedure for requesting an assembly with you.

You know your children best. Consider how your assemblies will link to your PSHE curriculum and your tutor time activities. Allow your tutors to be able to plan by sharing your assemblies and events calendar at the same time each half term with weekly updates.

Every assembly should go through a quality assurance process that ensures that each one is created with the appropriate thought and time, also allowing for the content to be properly checked for exemplary grammar and spelling. It may seem a little trite, but just checking any film clips and links are appropriately embedded will keep the assembly running smoothly and the audience engaged. There is nothing worse than being thrown as a presenter when your technology fails you and you can see the audience's concentration dissipate before your eyes. I always advise my heads of year to have a back-up plan for this instance but when outside visitors are presenting, checking their presentation works before the day ensures this shouldn't happen.

Consistency is key to ensuring key messages are delivered and understood across your year group. What do you want your students to know, believe and abide by? Decide on what you want your key messages to be and establish a standard set of slides that you will use each week. Having the same opening to your assembly will give it structure and your students will expect to be presented with certain information.

During the exam season, a dip in attendance and an increase in negative behaviour often occur when assemblies are not regularly kept. This is particularly prevalent during the main examination period. Be creative in your approach. Not every assembly needs to be a whole-year-group assembly. Do you have smaller spaces where you could meet a number of tutor groups together? Can you deliver assemblies via a broadcast or pre-recorded video link? These methods can help maintain standards until you can resume normal scheduling.

Tips to consider:

- Go and see what your different heads of year and senior leaders do in other assemblies to obtain and share ideas.
- Use a variety of delivery methods so your assemblies don't become too predictable. Stories, video clips, student-led assemblies, visitors or tutors can help to make it engaging.
- Link your assembly themes to current events to keep them up to date.
- Make a whole-year plan so you can map out the important messages at key times throughout the year.
- Wherever possible, share your schedule with your tutor team at least one week in advance so they can prepare their other tutor time activities accordingly.
- Create a central resource for assemblies with the other heads of year in your school. Sharing means less work for everyone.

## Chapter 13 takeaway

### Key points

- Bringing your whole year group together for a formal assembly is vitally important if you want to foster a strong sense of community within your year group. This is a great opportunity to reinforce your core values and ethos on a regular basis.
- A collective act of daily worship is an expectation of all schools in the UK. How you do this is up to each and every individual school, but the extent to which you promote the spiritual, moral, social and cultural development of your children will be judged by any school inspection team.

- Strategically planning the themes and content of your assemblies is vital if you want to get the most impact out of the time you have with your whole year group. By having a consistent structure for your assemblies and key messages important to your year group and school context that are regular fixtures of your assembly, this will stop negative messages for the minority being spread to the majority.

## Next steps

- **Read**

  Read *Secondary School Assemblies for Busy Teachers* by Mark and Luke Williams, Juliet Stafford and Shepherd Donna-Lynn for a collection of 'ready-to-go' topical presentations varying between five and 15 minutes in length.

- **Connect**

  Connect with other heads of year in your school to get ideas on assembly themes throughout the year. Share resources and ideas between you, so that you don't all have to reinvent the wheel.

- **Reflect**

  Reflect on assemblies that you have either delivered or have been lucky (or unlucky!) enough to have sat through. What made them great or not so great? Are there any assemblies that left a lasting positive impression on you from your own school days?

# 14

# Complexities for specific year groups

---

## CHAPTER OVERVIEW

In this chapter we will look at the complexities involved when leading these specific year groups:

- Year 7 – the year of transition
- Year 9 – the year of change
- Year 11 – the year of exams.

---

## Year 7 – the year of transition

One of the key pastoral roles in many secondary schools these days is head of Year 7. With transition from primary to secondary school increasingly being focussed on both pastoral and academic transition, the head of Year 7 role is fundamental to getting your students off to the very best start possible, both in the classroom and in the playground. For the vast majority of children, this will be the most significant change in their lifetime, so inevitably there will be a lot of worry and anxiety from not only the students but their parents as well. It is therefore essential for schools to develop extremely well-planned transition programmes that start well in advance of the students arriving in September. Due to this, many schools now structure their pastoral leadership system with a static head of Year 7 who is the constant face of transition, meaning that they can build links with primary schools over the years, fine-tuning their transition programme through experience, rather than a different person having a go at it each year.

Anyone who has been head of Year 7 will certainly tell you that it is a year like no other. Although you may not have the complex characters of stressed-out 16-year-olds to deal with as you would in Year 11, you'll certainly be kept on your toes by your enthusiastic and excited 11-year-olds. Here are some generic issues that most heads of Year 7 would tell you to expect.

## Anxiety

Although most students will naturally feel nervous about starting secondary school, there will always be a small percentage of students whose anxiety gets the better of them and continues to present itself well after the first morning of the first day. In my experience, this is sometimes accentuated by their parents. Like any individual situation you may deal with as a head of year, there is no silver bullet or textbook answer for this. However, the quicker you can identify any students where there is an issue, the better. An effective transition programme should have hopefully picked up any potential anxious students months in advance and steps should have already been taken to alleviate any concerns. This is where the familiar face of the head of Year 7 really pays dividends.

## *Friendships and social groups*

Naturally when children move up to secondary school, they lose friends (those moving to other schools) and pick up new friends along the way. However, this is not as straightforward as it sounds. In my experience of being head of Year 7, friendship issues are probably the most time-consuming part of your role. Not emotionally mature enough to handle these sudden changes in relationships happening around them, many Year 7 students end up being upset when their previous best friend from primary school finds new friends in their new classes. This can become even more significant when students create tight friendship groups and students are either excluded from a group because of a falling out with someone, or faced with tough choices over which group they want to be in.

## *Pecking order*

Most human beings feel the need to know where they are in a certain pecking order. For 11-year-old boys, this often means who is the 'hardest' boy in the year group. If you have a number of different primary schools sending students to your school, then inevitably there will be boys who have always held the 'title' of being the hardest in their school. Put these boys all together in a new school and there is bound to be some interesting physical encounters between them until they work out their new pecking order. The same can also sometimes be seen on the sports field or in the classroom. If you've always been told (or have thought) that you have been the best in your school at something, it can take some time to get used to the fact that there are others out there who are better than you and who are now in your class!

## *Ability setting*

Most students in primary school will have been taught for the majority of the time in a mixed-ability class. Although some primary schools try to teach literacy and numeracy to targeted sets of students based on ability, the general experience of education that primary students are used to is learning in a mixed-ability class where all their friends are. So, not only are students now moving to a new school in September, but they are also potentially moving to a whole new educational system. Suddenly they are being streamed into pathways or placed in ability sets for certain subjects. This can be quite a pressured situation for students who are in top sets. The pressure from the school, themselves or their parents to stay there can sometimes be too much to take for an 11-year-old who has just gone through the biggest change in their life so far. Explaining to parents why their son or daughter has been placed in a certain set is also extremely time-consuming. Lots of parents will feel like their child needs to be in the 'top set', without any understanding of the data that ranks another 30 or 40 students above them.

## *General organisation*

At primary school, most things are done for students. Equipment is quite frequently provided on desks, students don't need to remember an hourly timetable of lessons and they rarely move from room to room every hour. You can therefore understand why so many students lose items of equipment or forget where they are supposed to be in the first few weeks of school. I've lost count of the number of phone calls I've taken from parents of Year 7 students who have lost their brand-new PE kit inside the first half term. Quite often parents will ring up to complain that an item of uniform or PE kit has been stolen from their child, only to find that, in fact, the student has just left it in a classroom or on the school field after lunchtime. Being responsible for their own equipment is something that students learn to do, but unfortunately it takes time.

### Personal reflection

How good is your school transition programme? What structures are in place to ensure that students make the best possible start to life in Year 7?

_____

_____

_____

_____

What skills and qualities do you think you would need in order to be a static head of Year 7 in your school?

_____

_____

_____

_____

_____

# Year 9 – the year of change

In most schools, the head of Year 9 will have followed this year group through the school so far (potentially from Year 8 after taking them from the static head of Year 7 if there is one), and will possibly stay with them until they leave Year 11. This model is predominantly seen as the most beneficial for pastoral care, as the skill of a head of year is to really get to know their students. By having a new cohort of students every year, you can never really do this. The minute you feel like you've got to know them (and their parents), you are passing them on to someone else. Parents also like to see consistency in the pastoral leadership of the year group and like to know that the head of year has a thorough understanding of their child.

For lots of schools, GCSE options take place in Year 9. Big decisions are to be made over what you might study in the future, together with what your career aspirations might be. Things start to get serious when parents and students are discussing option choices and how it might affect where they go after they leave school. However, whilst all these big decisions are being taken, there are also some quite significant changes happening to their body at the same time. This can cause a rollercoaster of emotions and be the catalyst for some quite interesting behaviour in school. Being head of Year 9 has a very different set of challenges to being head of Year 7, but it's no less demanding; there's just a different set of issues to resolve.

## Puberty

Around this time in their life, most students will experience puberty. Although some may not show it on the outside with obvious changes to their appearance, there may be some significant physical and emotional changes happening on the inside. For some children, this can result in a dramatic change in behaviour, both in school and at home. One of the main reasons behind this change is because teenagers are starting to find their own independence, make their own decisions away from their parents and teachers who have always previously been the decision makers in their life. At the same time as this is happening, children of this age are increasingly aware of how others, especially their peers, see them. The desire to desperately try to fit in to their new social groups means that their peers often become much more important than parents or teachers when it comes to making decisions.

## *Relationships*

The middle years in a student's life in school can also be when more advanced relationships are formed. These relationships may be in the form of strong, lasting bonds with their close friends, or there's the possibility of intimate and sexual relationships with students in their peer group. These relationships can have a multitude of effects on the students, many of which can have significantly negative effects on their education. When best friends fall out or physical relationships break up, the aftermath can be devastating for young people, especially if it's the talk of the school. Add into the mix a student being pushed out of a friendship circle with whom they share all the same classes and you've got a lot of sweeping up to do as a head of year. Relationships can also be a negative distraction for some students whilst they are happily 'in love' for the first time. I've seen many young students absolutely smitten by a peer, and suddenly their focus on their school work takes a back seat, because they now have a new priority in their life.

## *Complacency*

Year 9 can also become a year of complacency for some students. Once they have got over their worries about transitioning from primary to secondary, settled themselves into their new surroundings and found their place in their new friendship groups, students can naturally begin to relax because they have now got their feet firmly under the table. Parents might notice this at home with their child not being as conscientious over homework or ensuring they have the right equipment in their bag. At school, teachers might notice changes in attitude and effort in the classroom, with students valuing school as a location that facilitates their social time, rather than a place where they come to learn. Luckily, as students generally become more mature and focussed on their education again, this begins to disappear.

## *Behaviour*

As we have already discussed in the section on puberty, many of the physical, intellectual and emotional changes that a child's body goes through at this time in their life can result in negative behaviour being displayed at home and in school. Most teachers will tell you that their Year 9 class is one of their most challenging classes because of that want (or need) to kick back against the system that has always made decisions for them. From instances of public insolence to outbursts of aggressive behaviour, Year 9 teachers probably see it all. As the head of year, this can be tricky to resolve with parents because they too may be struggling to cope with this sudden change in behaviour and may not have had the experience of dealing with it before. Your skill in managing these situations is therefore crucial so that you can reassure the parents that it might not be anything that they are doing wrong, but just the physical changes that their child is currently going through.

## Personal reflection

What strategies does your current school have in place to help students manage this period of physical and emotional change in their lives?

_____

_____

_____

_____

_____

How could you be more proactive in your approach to managing this change?

_____

_____

_____

_____

# Year 11 – the year of exams

For many students and their parents, everything they've done at both primary and secondary school has been building up to this point in time. Year 11 is always seen as the most important school year and one that may define a child's future based on how successful they are in their final examinations. The external pressure from parents to do better than they ever did can be a burden that students carry with them all year until they open that envelope on results day. Add to that the pressure from teachers for students to perform in line with their expectations so that schools achieve their own targets, and you begin to see how much external pressure some students feel. Without the strong emotional resilience and maturity that adults possess, this can make for an extremely personally challenging time for our students.

Due to the intensity of Year 11 and the similar knowledge of annual procedures and events (just like in Year 7), some schools now employ a static head of Year 11 to work in the exact same way as the static head of Year 7 that we discussed earlier in this chapter. Although the disadvantage you have is that you don't have an in-depth knowledge of every student, the advantage is that you are skilled in every aspect of the forthcoming year, knowing how to proactively support the year group through the obstacles ahead. In some schools where this approach is used, the assistant head of year or a non-teaching support worker from the year office still follows the year group through to support the new head of Year 11, so that you get the best of both worlds.

If you are taking on a new role as head of Year 11, or moving through with your year group into Year 11 for the first time, here are some of the pressure points that you might come across.

## *Stress*

With the increased pressure and intensity that students feel in Year 11, it is only natural that this will be displayed in the form of stress. Some students will be a nervous wreck and at your office door every day in floods of tears, whilst some students you will never need to worry about. The key is identifying which students will need your help and getting to them with support, care and advice before they come looking for it from you. For most students this will be the most stressful time they have ever experienced in their life and many will not have the coping strategies to be able to self-regulate their emotions. A great school and head of year will understand this and already have structures of support in place to help their students through this. It is also important to keep a close eye on any staff who seem to be passing their own stress of meeting their targets on to your students. As head of year, this might just be the year that your students need you the most.

## Study skills

Although effective schools should have already embedded great study skills from the minute that the students entered the building in Year 7, many students either have a lack of confidence about their ability to study for their exams, or simply do not know how to study effectively. Research around how we retain information tells us that the way we were probably taught to revise when we were at school (re-read our notes and copy them out) is probably the worst way to remember anything. So it is now up to us as leaders of our year groups to ensure we pass on the very best revision strategies to our students, so they have the best possible chance of being successful in their exams. Unfortunately, some of our students might not want to hear these messages and will try to take short cuts in their revision. Understanding how our students are revising through careful mentoring of key individuals who we know will need our advice is an important step in supporting them academically.

## Prom

Although the prom is supposed to be one of the most enjoyable aspects of our students' time with us in school, it can also prove to be one of the most stressful. Choosing what to wear, how to arrive and who to go with can send some students over the edge months in advance of the big evening. The pressure for parents to stump up hundreds of pounds on a prom outfit that may never be worn again can be quite intense. You only leave school once, so getting it right is vital, especially when you take into account the social pressure of fitting in with your friends. Expensive cars, matching accessories, spray tans and hairstyles all add up to a hefty bill for a student's parents. Many schools now use reward schemes in Year 11 to offset the cost of the prom ticket through attendance initiatives or good behaviour programmes. Some schools also have deals with local dress shops, hairdressers and beauty salons to provide students with the most cost-effective way to look a million dollars on their big night.

## Leaving

For some students, leaving school is something to look forward to, but for others it creates a level of uncertainty. Going off into the big wide world is exciting for some and terrifying for others. There are some students who will see the fast-approaching end of their time with you as a real worry because the warm, supportive and caring environment that you have provided them has been the only one of its kind in their life. School has been the safe place for them where boundaries are consistent and they know that they are being looked after. Leaving this environment will create a level of instability that they have only ever experienced over holiday periods, some of which have been nowhere near as positive as their time in school. Identifying these students can be hard though. They will rarely tell you this is what they are worried about, especially when the rest of their peer group are excited about the prospect of leaving school. Instead, this anxiety might present itself in other ways, such as sudden changes in behaviour and attitude. A great head of year will be able to put all of the pieces of the jigsaw together in order to get to the root of the problem and support the student in the most effective way.

## Personal reflection

What strategies does your current school employ in Year 11 to stop students from getting overly stressed about their forthcoming exams?

_____

_____

_____

_____

_____

What skills would you require to support a student through anxious times in Year 11? Have you got these skills? And if not, how can you acquire them?

_____

_____

_____

_____

_____

# Academic and pastoral transition

Making the switch to secondary school can be a daunting process, so schools need to have well-structured transition programmes to ensure all students settle into life at secondary school as quickly as possible. Lynette Harte reflects on why the head of Year 7 role is so important in helping students make a successful transition.

## PROFESSIONAL PERSPECTIVE: BEING HEAD OF YEAR 7

### By Lynette Harte, Former Head of Year at Stamford High School, now School Liaison Officer at Resilient Rutland

Being head of Year 7 is an absolute privilege. As I say to my Year 7 team, we can make such a huge difference to our youngest students as they start secondary school. When leading Year 7, be open and honest from the beginning. Any journey has its highs and lows, and starting secondary school is no different. So, as a starting point, we spread the message that Year 7 is an adventure we undertake together and along the way we will make mistakes, get lost, make friends, have harder times, try new things and be amazing in our own way.

My role in transition is a big one and this starts early. I think it is of real benefit to create the opportunity for primary children to visit secondary schools and of course for us to visit them. Start in Year 5 if you can. In the summer term, I make it a priority to go to primary schools and personally visit every single child who is joining us in September. This is a chance to find out what they like, dislike and are looking forward to. You also become a familiar face for when they start in September. Some big questions get asked at this early stage and it is a time to listen and reassure. Through the visits I start to put form groups together and pre-empt future friendships they don't even know about yet.

During visits, I liaise with teachers, pastoral leads and learning support colleagues to gather information for the academic and pastoral teams before September. This allows time to arrange additional individual transition activities if needed. We organise a transition day in June to include lessons and meeting form tutors and of course each other – it aims to cast aside worries before the summer. Try to look at things through the eyes of the children and gain their feedback. It has always been my priority to reflect on our transition process and look at how we can continue to improve. This is a real benefit of being a 'static' head of Year 7, as you can evaluate previous years and make necessary changes.

As a head of year, I have helped develop activities to assist friendship formation in those early weeks. I have found that getting students off timetable for a day early in that first term is great – allowing teambuilding and a lot of laughter. A head of Year 7 needs to be brave and think big – nothing cements relationships better than overnight camping and trying new things. The power of a school trip or the big outdoors is huge for Year 7, as it removes barriers to starting conversations and getting to know people.

Once friendships begin and the initial fear fades, our role shifts to assisting organisation. Secondary school can be so huge compared to the primary school that the students have come to know so well. There are so many teachers, books, equipment, rooms and homework to remember. We look closely at developing skills, planning, and organising bags and personal equipment. Never take anything for granted with transition – they might not all know the obvious and you need to bring them up to speed on routine, pace and expectation. We also help students understand how to manage friendship conflict and change because they cannot always sort things alone.

Finally, my role in transition is just as important with the parents to prepare them for the inevitable changes. Sending a welcome letter to introduce myself and outline key areas in transition is helpful, and an evening for new parents in June allows the answering of questions and to start to build those important relationships. A Year 7 Twitter feed, newsletter or blog also debunks myths and allows parents to feel part of the community. I have always placed great value on honest dialogue with parents. You gain feedback, learn more about the children and most importantly you can work together if crisis hits – which sadly it can.

As head of Year 7, every day is different. It is brilliant, rewarding and exhausting, but you can make such a difference if your transition and pastoral care are strong.

Here are my top tips for Year 7 transition:

1 Visit their primary schools and have them visit you. Remember the little things they tell you.
2 Liaise closely with your primary colleagues. They know the children so well.
3 Don't get caught in routine. No transition is ever the same.
4 Remember the parents. Communicate with them and help them manage this change too.
5 Get them off timetable. Get outside, try new things, take risks and build friendships.
6 Nurture the team around you – together you are an incredible energy. Lift each other daily.

---

## Chapter 14 takeaway

### Key points

- Successful transition to secondary school is fundamental to long-term student success. Great schools have highly effective transition programmes that start working with students in Year 6 and do everything they can to settle students into their new surroundings in Year 7.
- Understanding the physical, emotional and intellectual changes that teenagers go through is essential for an effective head of year. Not only will you need to support your students through these physical changes, but you may also have to support their parents too.

- Teenagers are often not emotionally resilient enough to cope with the pressures of terminal examinations that will decide their whole future. Being ready to cope with the tears, the frustrations and the euphoria of the life of a student in Year 11 might just be one of your biggest challenges too.

## Next steps

- **Read**

  Read *100 Ideas for Primary Teachers: Transition to Secondary School* by Molly Potter and *100 Ideas for Secondary Teachers: Revision* by John Mitchell for specific ideas on being head of year for both Year 7 and Year 11.

- **Connect**

  If you are taking on a new head of year role, speak to other heads of year in your school about the specific issues that they faced when their year group were the same age as yours. The more ready you can be for the challenges ahead, the better.

- **Reflect**

  Reflect on your own teaching experiences of teaching specific year groups. What makes them different from one another? What different skills do you need to employ in the classroom for different year groups? And how can you adapt these skills to be a successful head of year for a specific year group?

# References

Ainsworth, P. (2016), *Bloomsbury CPD Library: Middle Leadership*. London: Bloomsbury Education.

Andrews, J., Robinson, D. and Hutchinson, J. (2017), 'Closing the gap? Trends in educational attainment and disadvantage'. London: Education Policy Institute, https://epi.org.uk/publications-and-research/closing-gap-trends-educational-attainment-disadvantage

Blyth, E. and Milner, J. (1999), *Improving School Attendance*. Abingdon: Routledge.

Cowley, S. (2014), *Getting the Buggers to Behave*. London: Bloomsbury Education.

Department for Education (2013), 'Religious education (RE) in academies', https://webarchive.nationalarchives.gov.uk/20130903174355/http://education.gov.uk/schools/leadership/typesofschools/academies/open/a00225252/religious-education-academies

Department for Education (2016), 'The link between absence and attainment at KS2 and KS4: 2013/14 academic year', https://assets.publishing.service.gov.uk/government/uploads/system/uploads/attachment_data/file/509679/The-link-between-absence-and-attainment-at-KS2-and-KS4-2013-to-2014-academic-year.pdf

Department for Education (2018a), 'Pupil absence in schools in England: 2016 to 2017', www.gov.uk/government/statistics/pupil-absence-in-schools-in-england-2016-to-2017

Department for Education (2018b), 'Schools, pupils and their characteristics: January 2018', www.gov.uk/government/statistics/schools-pupils-and-their-characteristics-january-2018

Department for Education (2019a), 'Keeping children safe in education', https://assets.publishing.service.gov.uk/government/uploads/system/uploads/attachment_data/file/835733/Keeping_children_safe_in_education_2019.pdf

Department for Education (2019b), 'Special
    educational needs: Analysis and summary of data
    sources', www.gov.uk/government/publications/
    sen-analysis-and-summary-of-data-sources
Dix, P. (2017), *When the Adults Change, Everything Changes*.
    Carmarthen: Crown House.
Halton Borough Council (2013), 'Guidelines for collective worship
    2017-2018', www4.halton.gov.uk/Pages/EducationandFamilies/
    PDFs/Schools/sacre/HaltonGuidelinesforCollectiveWorship.pdf
Mitchell, J. (2016), *100 Ideas for Secondary Teachers: Revision*.
    London: Bloomsbury Education.
O'Leary, L. (2019), *100 Ideas for Secondary Teachers:
    Interventions*. London: Bloomsbury Education.
Potter, M. (2015), *100 Ideas for Primary Teachers: Transition to
    Secondary School*. London: Bloomsbury Education.
Potter, M. (2016), *100 Ideas for Secondary Teachers: Tutor Time*.
    London: Bloomsbury Education.
Rubin, G. (2011), *The Happiness Project*. New York, NY: Harper.
Sobel, D. (2018), *Narrowing the Attainment Gap*. London:
    Bloomsbury Education.
Sobel, D. (2019), *Leading on Pastoral Care*. London: Bloomsbury
    Education.
Social Mobility and Child Poverty Commission (2014), 'State of
    the nation 2014: Social mobility and child poverty in Great
    Britain', https://assets.publishing.service.gov.uk/government/
    uploads/system/uploads/attachment_data/file/365765/State_
    of_Nation_2014_Main_Report.pdf
Taylor, C. (2012), 'Improving attendance at school'.
    London: Department for Education, www.gov.uk/government/
    publications/improving-attendance-at-school
The Bell Foundation (2015), 'EAL and educational
    achievement', www.bell-foundation.org.uk/research-report/
    eal-educational-achievement
Williams, M., Williams, L., Stafford, J. and Donna-Lynn, S. (2015),
    *Secondary School Assemblies for Busy Teachers - Volume 2*.
    Castlebar: Checkpoint Press.

# Index